W9-CBN-472

GEORGIA
LAND OF MANY DREAMS

First published in Great Britain 1984 by Colour Library Books Ltd.

Published 1984 by Crescent Books, distributed by Crown Publishers, Inc.
Colour separations by Llovet S.A., Barcelona, Spain.
Printed and bound in Barcelona, Spain by Rieusset and Eurobinder.
ISBN 0 517 436418
h g f e d c b a

GEORGIA
LAND OF MANY DREAMS

Text by Margaret Shakespeare

Featuring the Photography of Julian Essam

Produced by
TED SMART and DAVID GIBBON

CRESCENT BOOKS
NEW YORK

Georgia's story reaches back to the prehistory of its native Indian peoples. The Creek, Guale, Cherokee, Yamasi, Cusabo, and other tribes lived in its Appalachian Mountain regions, the red clay piedmont, on the inland plains and islands along the coast.

School children all across this state learn about its founding in 1733 as colony number thirteen, last in the group of British establishments in the New World which later became the United States. They memorize facts about its longest river (the Chattahoochee, 436 mostly unnavigable miles), unusually large number of counties (159, second only to Texas), tallest mountain (Brasstown Bald rising 4,784 feet), oldest natural gorge in North America (Tallulah Gorge, 2,000 feet deep, where Karl Wallenda made an historic tightrope walk), state flower (Cherokee Rose), state bird (Brown Thrasher) and so on. They write essays about people who lived and worked here like Crawford W. Long (the first physician known to have used ether as an anesthetic), Alexander H. Stephens (Vice President of the Confederacy), Joel Chandler Harris (journalist and creator of Uncle Remus), and Eli Whitney (inventor of the cotton gin). President Franklin D. Roosevelt gets a prominent footnote since he spent so much time during his presidency at the "Little White House" he built near Warm Springs, Georgia, where he took therapy for polio.

Travelers through the state on the network of interstate highways, back country roads, suburban and city streets, see a modernistic skyline reaching up and, symbolically, into the future. Small towns snug against peach orchards, chicken farms, and cornfields; by the sea lie quiet beaches and unspoilt marshlands; elsewhere, humble little mountains are covered with the brilliant colors of autumn or glow with green during the warm months. Farmers around Vidalia harvest their sweet onions in May and June. Apple orchards let you pick your own fruit when the air is crisp in November. Truck farmers take their fresh greens, okra, watermelons, and tomatoes directly to consumer markets in the cities. Every roadside stand sells sacks of Georgia pecans and Georgia peanuts.

Georgia holds within her boundaries contrasts in both nature and man. Society is at once urban and rural; progressive and conservative; looking ahead and preserving the past.

Atlanta, the Big A, largest city and capital of the state, quickly achieved a regional status in business, economics, and transportation that propelled it forward to leadership in both culture and education. The city visibly aspires to continue an established pattern of pacesetting and rising importance in national and international circles. Hardly anyone here can claim to be a native. The citizens come from all over the world, which gives many of its neighborhoods transient characteristics. The whole city moves about tethered to its automobiles; walking is what you do with a dog.

Atlanta reached the lowest point in its brief history over a hundred years ago; indeed the Battle of Atlanta nearly marked the point of no return. A group of artists recreated the ghastly scene on canvas hung in the round. With the addition in the foreground of three-dimensional figures and landscaping, the Cyclorama can be seen in Atlanta's Grant Park. The display rivals Margaret Mitchell's *Gone with the Wind* for a classic image of the city's reduction to ashes.

Indeed, the uninitiated may imagine Georgia as still the land of Scarlett O'Hara's Tara. The era of plantations did shape economic development in the South, but the reality and romance of those times evaporated long ago. Today Georgians often have to answer a tourist's query about where the cotton fields are, but they themselves live with contemporary problems of pollution, transportation, urban growth, inflation, and taxes.

Since those "good old days", Georgians have taken strides forward in politics, government, and social change. The great civil rights leader Martin Luther King, Jr., a native Atlantan, won the Nobel Peace Prize and some of the nation's most far-reaching victories over racial discrimination. He came from a black middle-class community that had produced many well-known figures. A cluster of institutions – Atlanta University, Clark College, Morehouse College, Spelman College, Morris Brown College – in the southwest section of the city educated generations of black students, many of whom went on to become known nationally. Besides King, State Senator Julian Bond, former Mayor Maynard Jackson, and Andrew Young, present Mayor and former United States Ambassador to the United Nations, among others, came from this tradition. Black enterprise has centered around "Sweet" Auburn Avenue since the turn of the century. Some have called it the "richest Negro street in the world."

In recent years, Georgians have taken more interest in their heritage. They're now willing to widen the circle and include backgrounds that might not quite match their own family trees.

In 1966, an idealistic young teacher named Eliot Wigginton joined the faculty of the Rabun Gap-Nacoochee School up in the north Georgia mountains. He took on the unenviable job of teaching English to the ninth and tenth graders. Within six weeks the kids had burnt his desk, scribbled graffiti all over their own, armed themselves with thumbtacks, water pistols, and pocket knives. Feeling that things weren't quite going his way but not yet ready to surrender to an adolescent zoo, Wigginton offered them a chance to start a magazine. He observed that this rural culture passed along information about itself from one generation to the next orally. The magazine would be the forum through which the children would collect ghost stories, recipes, planting instructions, hunting tales, log cabin blueprints, histories of burial customs, quilting patterns, snake lore and "other affairs of plain living," edit the material and produce articles, photographs, drawings; whatever would tell the stories of their lives and legacy.

The first issue of *Foxfire* sold out two printings within a week. Wigginton had launched an idea that taught young students how to research and write and run a business but, just as important, it gave them a sense of themselves and their families that they could never have gotten from a textbook. *Foxfire* telling about planting by the zodiac signs and midwifery in remote mountain counties where there are no doctors, and other vignettes of everyday life, now goes to subscribers in all fifty states. It has spawned over a half dozen Foxfire books, lecture tours for Wigginton and the kids, documentary films, a Broadway play, grants for the school, and a lot of native pride.

At the other end of Georgia, heritage has been preserved and put on public display in quite another manner. The city of Savannah, oldest municipality in the state, made itself keeper of architectural and urban history. The streets, filled with restored houses and squares, seem like an out-of-doors museum and, indeed, many visitors refer to the historic district as America's favorite walking tour. It has gone from ugly duckling to a showplace through a remarkable restoration effort, which has taken over thirty years. Architecture students from schools all over the world come here to do field work in restoration and to study fine examples of English Regency and Early Federal buildings. Savannah's lovely blocks of row houses star in the movies, too.

Hollywood discovered this authentic southern backdrop and has used it in such films as *East of Eden*.

Directors and producers also found rugged outdoor locations in the state which were to their liking. The Chattooga River in North Georgia, great for white water rafting, appeared in the Burt Reynolds' movie *Deliverance*. Reynolds, originally from Waycross, Georgia, has directed and starred in a number of films made almost entirely on Georgia sites. His *Sharkey's Machine* features downtown Atlanta, particularly the new Peachtree Plaza Hotel. The scouts for *The Scottsboro Boys* found a courthouse in middle Georgia which suited their requirements. Movie-making has been something of a boon for the state. To encourage the industry, and to create work for more Georgians, the government set up the Georgia Film Commission. According to some reports, Georgia now ranks just behind California and New York in movie-related activity.

Communications entrepreneur Ted Turner put Georgia on the national television scene, too. He introduced his cable channel to viewers all over the United States after it had become popular in Atlanta for its full schedule of old movies. Since maverick Turner owns the Atlanta Braves franchise he, of course, makes it possible for fans wherever they are to see the games.

In Georgia, people who want to make their own adventure, rather than watch it in a movie or on a television screen, can head out in almost any direction. Winter resorts in the mountains, some only an hour's drive north of Atlanta, accommodate downhill skiers. Summer outdoorsmen can find trails and campsites in this same area. The Appalachian Trail, which follows the mountain range up to Maine, starts in Georgia at Springer Mountain. It takes three to six months to complete the hike along the well-worn path. By April the weather has usually warmed up enough to make mountain nights in a sleeping bag tolerable and safe. Caretakers keep the Trail clear and well marked, and towns usually lie within shouting distance.

If your idea of sports is lying back and waiting for the fish to bite, Georgia has plenty of stocked lakes. The largest, Lake Sidney Lanier, features a planned recreation resort with horseback riding, golf, swimming, picnic grounds, playgrounds, and boats – kayaks, canoes, catamarans, sail boats, pontoons, paddle boats, and houseboats – for hire. This man-made lake became Atlanta's weekend cottage community in the 1950s, and on a Sunday evening, westbound traffic backed up Interstate-85 worse than at 5 o'clock rush hour.

If you'd just like to watch seasoned golf pros do all the work, try to get a coveted ticket to the Master's Tournament, held each April in Augusta, Georgia. Georgia counts among its beloved native sportsmen Bobby Jones, who won the prestigious Masters, a classic Georgia event, several times. The course itself was a favorite of President Dwight Eisenhower.

Georgians will tell you immediately, when asked just who has done what, and when, within its borders. Georgia is concerned with appearances and it invests in its image. It wants to be remembered for the merits of its natural resources and it promotes past and present achievements that reflect the state in a pleasant light, whether you come here to work or live or play, or you're just changing at Atlanta's mammoth airport. Somehow the myths inevitably persist anyway.

Georgians don't like being reminded that their ancestors may have been debtors who had been imprisoned in England as common criminals because the facts can be easily misconstrued. In fact, the story of Georgia's founding has gotten a bit out of hand in some of its popular versions. Eighteenth-century British law allowed that anyone who had overspent his credit could be thrown into prisons which reeked of death and disease. Once interred in these uninhabitable pest bins, a prisoner found himself hopelessly confronted with having to bribe his way to freedom. The longer he remained unable to pay up, even if the original debt had been forgiven, the more heinous his incarceration.

A man named James Edward Oglethorpe, who had been

elected to Parliament, began a sanctioned investigation into prison conditions. He believed that there had to be a reasonable alternative and sought to provide poor people with a fresh start. He had a personal interest in the investigation because his architect friend, Robert Castell, had been tossed into Fleet Prison by his creditors, and had died there in a smallpox ward. Just about the time that Parliament had passed the Debtors Act of 1730, King George II signed a charter to establish a colony between South Carolina (an English colony) and Florida (Spanish territory). Oglethorpe, as one of the new colony's trustees, volunteered to lead a group of carefully-selected, less fortunate men and women – who might otherwise have found a miserable end in prison – and others who sought to create a new life abroad.

The rest of the story is a little happier, although starting from scratch – felling trees, constructing living quarters, clearing and seeding farm land, fighting Spaniards – didn't make for the most comfortable life style. The city they started went on to become an exemplary historic showpiece. Today, Savannah is one of the images Georgia seeks to present to others.

In looking at a large and diverse piece of real estate that packs in several centuries of living, one usually comes away with a few impressions that stand out. Those of us who have spent several important years in an area develop our own prejudices for or against the environment. We participate in a community or not, and our subjective observations may be quite intimate. Feelings grow and change with the passage of time, and some places compel us not to ignore them. Therefore, from a panoramic Georgia album, we have selected three scenes by which to introduce the state.

The Golden Isles tell an extraordinary series of historical tales, and they exist as a living laboratory, unlocking some secrets of the future to scientists and environmentalists who study their protected and preserved nature. Savannah, a trove of man-made past, cleaned itself up, dusted itself off and straightened up the archives a few years ago. Its original story, and that of its remarkable reemergence, interlock. Perhaps you should take the tour, at least in your mind's eye, along paths laid by Oglethorpe and others. Opposite in character, but as much a representative part of Georgia, Atlanta conveys the image and spirit of the future for the whole southeastern region. It lives by a different historical time clock and thrives at a faster pace.

Welcome to Georgia. Enjoy, and y'all come back.

The Golden Isles – linked to an intricate and curious past and enjoying a low-profile present – extend 150 miles along Georgia's shore, the entire Atlantic coastline of the state. Beaches in neighboring South Carolina, to the north, and Florida, to the south, beckon sun worshippers, boaters, fishermen, and golfers. They crowd thousands of condominiums, hotels, motels, restaurants, marinas, parks, and campsites. Developers make fortunes from Hilton Heads and Amelia Islands, and the tourists bring in millions of dollars in revenue for the state. Yet most of the exquisitely picturesque sandy shores of Georgia don't, and won't, host the Surf City crowd. Nearly all of the dozen or so of Georgia's barrier islands can still be reached only by water. But that's not the reason the population stays away. The answer lies amid a complex web of historical, ecological, environmental, cultural, and financial reasons.

Not too long after 1492, the Spanish sailed to the mainland of the North American continent and began establishing permanent settlements: towns to hold their land claims and missions to minister to the Indians. In 1566, on present-day St. Catherines Island, Georgia, they chose a spot for a mission called Santa Catalina, which was probably the first mission in North America. Its position was strategically midway between their posts at Parris Island, South Carolina, and St. Augustine, Florida. Guale (pronounced wally) Indians inhabited this fertile island at the time the Jesuits came to live among them. In ensuing years natives forced the Spanish settlers to abandon Santa

Catalina more than once. The priests kept journals, some extant and much studied by scholars and historians, describing the insubordinance of the Guale. After the Jesuits left for good, Franciscan missionaries arrived in 1597 and stayed on intermittently, though not always peacefully, until 1680.

Meanwhile, in 1670 the English had settled Charles Town in South Carolina. To assert territorial rights in the southeast coastal region, three hundred British and Indians combined forces against three dozen Spanish at Santa Catalina. Surprisingly, the lesser group prevailed, but they decided to quit the island anyway and departed, taking the Guale with them to the area of St. Augustine. With no trace of these Indians remaining in the region in which they had been indigenous, the Guale of St. Catherines Island have been known as the lost tribe of Georgia.

With the demise of the Spanish the islands then reverted to their former quiet existence as hunting and fishing grounds for the Creeks and other tribes who still lived in what is now south Georgia. When General James Edward Oglethorpe came to the New World in 1733 with a deed to all land between the Savannah and Altamaha Rivers, he set up certain territories for Indian use (by all accounts treating them more fairly than had earlier European settlers) and also built up fortifications on the islands to protect the fledging colony from the ever-present threat of Spanish invasion from the south. Fort Frederica, which he erected on St. Simons Island, was the most expensive British stronghold ever constructed on this continent. Its remains are now open as a National Monument.

Both sides coveted this property called the "Debatable Land," and skirmishes between them continued until British troops finally won decisively at the Battle of Bloody Marsh on St. Simons in 1742. Oglethorpe and his men abandoned Fort St. Simons as the Spanish invaded the south end of the island. British soldiers from Fort Frederica met the opposition as they advanced inland. After a clash the British retreated, for all appearances leaving the enemy with no more resistance. However, Scottish Highlanders and other British troops allied with Indians took cover in the surrounding woods and made a surprise attack, soundly defeating the Spanish and crucially determining undisputed and permanent British authority and influence over the islands and the entire southeast.

Soon it remained for the British to decide exactly who had rights to three much sought-after islands: Ossabaw, St. Catherines and Sapelo. Mary Musgrove – a half-breed Creek princess – and her third husband, Thomas Bosomworth, claimed the Indians had granted them this land from among Indian properties designated by Oglethorpe. When colonial trustees questioned the exercise of these land rights, Bosomworth took his case to court in England. The controversy – including arguments over payment to Mary Musgrove for goods and services to British troops in Georgia, use of slave labor, etc. – dragged on for over a decade. An eventual decision gave St. Catherines outright to Princess Mary and Thomas Bosomworth and also allowed them to benefit from sale of Ossabaw and Sapelo. Grey Elliott bought Ossabaw for £1,300 and soon sold it for the same amount. In 1760 Elliott also purchased Sapelo for £725. So much for pre-Revolutionary War real estate values. These deeds marked the beginnings of private ownership of the Golden Isles – all except St. Simons – which largely continues today.

Blackbeard Island hooks around the northeast corner of Sapelo, separated only by a little creek, and in property transfers the two were usually linked as one entry. Although all the islands located along the strategic Georgia coast boast pirate legends, Blackbeard, as its name indicates, has the most colorful association with seafaring scalawags. Many of the tinier islands – there are hundreds – further toward the mainland have self-revealing appellations. One that served as a smugglers' hideaway is still called Hush-Your-Mouth Island.

In the early 1700s Edward Teach, better known as

Blackbeard, preyed on the thriving Atlantic shipping trade from the Caribbean into New England. The Georgia islands – with virgin forests, marshlands and thick brush – provided perfect concealment for the gold, silver and precious cargo that Teach and his compatriots seized from Spanish galleons and other merchant ships. Teach, who claimed to be the brother of the devil, would bombard unsuspecting vessels with the strength of forty guns from his *Queen Anne's Revenge* and then storm aboard, waving cutlass, flashing pistols and knives, as much a swashbuckler as a pirate can be who ties his long, braided hair and beard with ribbons. The spoils he then deposited on his island stronghold, declaring that he or the devil – the survivor – would be heir to the booty. Blackbeard's maritime theatrics finally got him dramatically decapitated after some shipboard hand-to-hand combat with Lieutenant Robert Maynard just off the coast of North Carolina. Ever since, rumor has persisted that his loot lies buried on the island bearing his pseudonym. So far as anyone has been able to prove the only things hidden in the sands of Blackbeard Island are dozens of eggs, the size and shape of ping pong balls, which are laid in nests at night by huge sea turtles. The turtles and their fellow creatures of the island's waters, marshlands, forests, and brush, have remained protected since 1914 – except perhaps from Blackbeard's ghost – in a wildlife preserve created by the federal government.

Cumberland, furthest south of the Golden Isles, most recently received government safeguarding. With its seventeen-mile stretch of undeveloped beach, peculiar changing dune structure, inland marshes, dense semi-tropical pine forests, herds of wild Spanish horses and diminutive Sicilian donkeys, this land across the intracoastal waterway from St. Marys, Georgia, became a National Seashore in 1972. Hardly the setting for a lavish resort hotel, cottages to accommodate five hundred guests, bowling alleys, a shooting gallery, a dance hall with live orchestra, and other entertainment, with a daily steamer service from Brunswick, Georgia. The good life enjoyed by an elite few lasted on Cumberland, as on neighboring Jekyll, until about the time of World War II.

Oglethorpe, the man responsible for planning and then defending young Georgia, made the first hunting lodge – called Dungeness – on Cumberland near the south end. Within a few decades royal grants gave parts of the island to various English families and, in 1768, an advertisement offering 7,500 acres for sale described the land as "fit for corn, rice, indigo, and cotton, and with a quality of live oak and pine for shipbuilding. Also extraordinary range for cattle, hogs, and horses." One of the largest plantations that flourished here later proved to be among the most prosperous in the state. The Stafford Plantation, occupying nearly a third of Cumberland – internally divided into two separate working farms, which created a healthy rivalry among workers – steadily reaped an outstanding annual crop.

The Dungeness name passed on to several successive estates located on, or near, the original hunting lodge site. General Nathanael Greene's family built a magnificent four-story mansion, where they lived year-round and entertained lavishly. Of course, when guests traveled great distances overland, and then by boat to an Atlantic wilderness island, they enjoyed lengthy visits in comfortable quarters. Private estates were designed and built to include generous guest facilities. The Greenes enjoyed plenty of famous company over the years: President George Washington in 1791, and General "Lighthorse" Harry Lee who died at Dungeness in 1818. Generations of Greenes and their heirs (the Shaws and Nightingales) stayed here with their families until the time of the Civil War, when nearly all island plantations were abandoned.

The attractive barrier islands lay exposed, free game for all manner of despoilers during the turmoil of the War. When, and if, owners returned to their properties that had once functioned virtually as small empires, they found great houses in ruins and the fields neglected and overgrown. An era and all its prosperity, style, and special *joie de vivre* had passed away. The aftermath of war and Reconstruction only added to the pain and readjustment. Time had washed monuments and memories into oblivion and most antebellum families of the Golden Isles chose to forsake them forever.

So by 1882, when Thomas Carnegie bought both Dungeness and the Stafford Plantation, civilization had deserted Cumberland for almost twenty-five years. The new Dungeness mansion constructed by Carnegie, with its gables and turrets, comfortable verandas and its focal fountain, became quite a social gathering place again. Stables housed horses, carriages, ponies for children and Russian bear hounds for hunting parties. Guests, brought over from the Georgia mainland by boat, and later by plane, could play golf or go boating or fishing.

Events of the twentieth century – primarily World War II – forced eventual abandonment of the luxurious island lifestyle. Estates like Dungeness, and the sumptuous hotel property on the north end of Cumberland, fell into eventual ruin. The Carnegies' great house burned down in 1959. When the Department of the Interior took custody of the island, they left it all as it was, including the ruins, the dunes, forests, and marshes. Still accessible only by water, park rangers take limited numbers of visitors over to Cumberland on day trips. They enjoy sharing the stories and lore of a barrier island that appears nearly the way it did to Spanish padres over four hundred years ago.

Sapelo, St. Catherines, and Ossabaw fared similarly. After British courts settled Mary Musgrove's case, and Sapelo and Ossabaw were sold – starting them on the protective course of private ownership – Mary lived on St. Catherines for a few years with her husband Thomas Bosomworth. Upon her death he sold the island to Button Gwinnett, later to win fame as a signer of the Declaration of Independence, and Gwinnett here enjoyed the life of a gentleman planter and politician. When he died suddenly at the age of forty two from a wound suffered in a duel, half the St. Catherines estate went to his family and the other half reverted to Bosomworth as payment for financial obligations. Gwinnett's wife and daughter survived him only briefly; Bosomworth's heirs lived out the century on the island.

In 1800 Jacob Waldburg, its new owner, developed two large plantations, and his tenure here – interrupted by the Civil War – continued until he sold it in 1872. Curious circumstances toward the end of the War turned some of these lands, including St. Catherines, into a separate island nation. Newly freed slaves had followed General William T. Sherman into Savannah on his destructive march to the sea. Having nothing else to offer, the Union leader let them take over crumbling coastal estates and plantations to the south of the port city. Tunis Campbell proclaimed himself governor of St. Catherines and maintained his position until evicted by Federal troops.

The next construction on the island was by purchaser John J. Rauers who, at the end of the nineteenth century, constructed a fine country house and game preserve for himself. Miraculously, the house Button Gwinnett had occupied still stood when, in 1927, ownership changed to Howard Coffin (who already owned Sapelo), C.M. Keys and James Willson. They remodelled the old gabled cottage, adding a wing, at the same time preserving the original mantel, stair railing, hand-pegged floor, and other eighteenth-century features. Keys soon became sole owner and then sold St. Catherines to Edward J. Noble in 1943.

By now it had flourished into a paradise island for animals, including herds of Black Angus cattle, sable antelopes, and grevy zebra. In recent years title has been transferred to the private Noble Foundation. St. Catherines continues as a sponsored refuge and survival center for endangered wild animals brought here from all over the world. The New York Zoological Society administers programs for the protection of such rarities as a herd of hartebeests, the only antelopes of their kind in North America.

Presently the wildlife shares St. Catherines with another breed – archaeologists from the American Museum of Natural History and other institutions engaged in locating and excavating sites of early Spanish occupation, prehistoric villages, burial grounds and other Indian artifacts. To date they have identified the location of the Santa Catalina church of 1566. Field research has revealed hundreds of Indian and Spanish graves within the walls of the church, many of the remains uncovered having precious metal medallions and pieces of shroud intact. With brand-new research techniques, teams of primary investigators can now determine much more about the lives of the Guale Indians, that so-called lost tribe, especially during the initial contact period.

Ossabaw, to the north of St. Catherines, and Sapelo, to the south, function today as wildlife sanctuaries as well. Both had served the Spanish perhaps as early as 1687. Written records describe gardens producing an abundance of peaches, figs, oranges, onions, and artichokes; ruins of forts, missions, and dwellings have also been found. Prior to English colonization and their subsequent sale to Grey Elliot, these islands earned a widespread reputation as rich hunting grounds. In short order Mr. Elliott resold them separately, and soon they flourished in the plantation tradition of the Golden Isles.

Five Frenchmen shared ownership of Sapelo. Ultimately, however, only Monsieur and Madame de Boisfeuillet, and then the Marquis de Montalet, established estates: Bourbon and Le Chatelet, respectively. De Montelet had the idea that he would find truffles somewhere on this lush island. Alas! He searched about with leashed pigs to no avail. Ruins of his house, which black slaves called "Chocolate", remain on the north end of Sapelo.

Thomas Spalding, from St. Simons, eventually bought most of the island. He designed a plantation house to be built low to the ground, with walls three feet thick so it would withstand the wind-lashing of hurricanes and other tropical storms that attack from the sea. A native of this coastal region, Spalding traveled the world. As an agriculturalist, he developed a great knowledge of cotton and wrote on the history of its cultivation for profit, as well as other treatises encouraging farmers in the area to diversify and rotate crops for improved yields. He was a pioneer in the exploiting and promoting of Georgia's sugar cane industry. In addition, he attended to business and political matters successfully, serving two terms in the United States Congress.

The overseer at Spalding's South End plantation was as much a special and charming character as his master. Bu Allah, Ben-Ali or Bul-ali (his various names), a Mohammedan who always wore a cap fashioned like a fez, spoke a familial dialect as well as French and English. He helped arm and defend Sapelo against the British in the War of 1812 and apparently left to posterity a small volume of Arabic writings in his own hand, which is noted as a very rare example of Afro-American work. Legends of Bu Allah lived on for decades on Sapelo, told and retold by his many descendants.

The Spalding family stayed on for several generations, absenting themselves from South End on the island only during the Civil War. Of course, life had changed dramatically by the later years of the nineteenth century and even rebuilding the main house was impractical. Sapelo fell into divided ownership again and served primarily as a recreational hunting ground.

When American industrialist Howard Coffin bought it in 1912 he renovated the Spalding mansion right away. Then he set about to create a great and lavish working plantation: fields were cultivated, wells drilled, 2,500 head of cattle set to range, horses stabled, and boats docked. Then, in 1925, he transformed South End into a palatial spread with landscaped gardens, outdoor reflecting pools, indoor swimming pools, and examples of fine sculpture – all the plushest appointments. The Coffins dazzled the most distinguished crowds of guests on the Atlantic coast: the Herbert Hoovers, President and Mrs. Calvin Coolidge, and Charles Lindbergh.

Tobacco magnate R.J. Reynolds bought the island paradise in 1933 and maintained it much as it had been for some twenty years. Then he began sharing his playground in philanthropic gestures, establishing an educational boys' camp, a school for island residents, and a marine research labratory.

The State of Georgia bought Sapelo in two separate parcels. The Marine Institute continues studies, seminars, and other programs at the South End House; Duplin River National Estuarine Sanctuary guards a unique six-mile tidal river used as a laboratory. The state also sponsors guided tours of Sapelo. The beaches, marshlands, and wildlife are all preserved in an unspoiled ecosystem.

A similar arrangement of government and private forces protects Ossabaw, the other island originally bought by Grey Elliott. Over the centuries inhabitants cultivated the land and produced rich crops of indigo and then cotton. Sea island cotton, a superior product, had twice the market value of ordinary cotton in the nineteenth century. Forests supplied a large amount of shipbuilding timber throughout the century. Primary among Ossabaw's succession of owners, several generations of Morels established a plantation empire to rival any other. Family members built several flourishing plantations and lived in a dichotomous world of luxury and primitivism. The first Morels freed the slaves of Ossabaw and paid them wages for their labor. When they finally felt forced to sell the property after the Civil War it had belonged to the family for over a century.

The Philadelphia Wanamakers, when they were exclusive owners, turned the land back into hunting grounds for relaxation and pleasure. In 1924, Dr. H.N. Torrey of Michigan purchased an Ossabaw inhabited by wild cattle and hogs. He made it once again a plantation paradise, with recreational facilities from the natural resources: grazing herds of cattle, conservative lumbering from great coastal forests, an excellent stock of hunting game and fish. He also encountered the same limitations as had several generations of island settlers. Ships brought over materials for the construction of a mansion that took years. Stones necessary for fireplaces and chimneys were especially precious, since the barrier islands do not have the required rock.

Descendants of the Torreys recently chose to turn over Ossabaw to a private foundation as an artists' retreat in the midst of a wilderness preserve. Scientists, students, and nature organizations also engage in sponsored projects that relate to conserving and knowing more about the ecosystem, which includes salt and freshwater marshes, freshwater ponds, forests of ancient live oaks, dogwood, wild azaleas, palm and magnolia trees, a thriving deer population, and other wonders of this semitropical island environment.

Government agencies and respective foundations administering Ossabaw, St. Catherines, Sapelo, Blackbeard, and Cumberland strictly control access to these barrier islands. Scout troops and other campers vie for the coveted few sanctioned campsites. Water taxis for day trips run on limited schedules. Generally hunting and fishing are prohibited, but an occasional lifting of deer hunting restrictions helps to control and balance the cervine population.

Three islands in the Georgia coastal chain – Jekyll, St. Simons, and Sea island, popularly referred to as the Golden Isles – have less stringent regulations and more development. Historically, at one time or another all the barrier islands together have been called "The Golden Isles." Today, the caption refers sometimes to the whole chain and sometimes to just these three that are better known. A few people erroneously believe the term "golden" stems from the bastion of great wealth and fame that isolated itself in this tiny part of the Atlantic seaboard in the late nineteenth and early twentieth centuries. Or that it harks back strictly to gold hidden here in the caches of pirates. However, Scottish nobleman Robert Montgomery probably first used the appellation formally in 1717 when he described in a *Discourse Concerning the Design'd Establishment of a New Colony*, natural virtues that had earned the "well deserved Denomination of the Golden Islands." Montgomery's treatise was part of an unrealized plan for a "Margravate of Azilia" to include Ossabaw, St. Catherines, Sapelo, and St. Simons.

Although Montgomery's Utopia remained but an idea, a group of American millionaires who sought an isolated spot of unexcelled natural beauty in an ideal climate, chose Jekyll Island for the site of their exclusive resort club. The Rockefellers, Vanderbilts, Cranes, Morgans, Goulds, Astors, Goodyears, McCormicks, Biddles, Whitneys, Macys, Pulitzers and others, then representing about a sixth of the world's wealth, bought the island for $125,000 in 1886 from descendants of Christopher Poulain duBignon. The Frenchman and his family, sole owners for nearly one hundred years, had successfully raised cotton on their plantation there.

The Jekyll Island Club, as the reclusive monied elite called themselves, sealed off their clubhouse (which had stained-glass windows designed and installed by Louis Comfort Tiffany), cottages, fabulous duned golf course, hunting forests (stocked with deer, turkey, quail, English pheasant, and wild boar) and other amenities – particularly their social activities – from the rest of the world. For the fifty-six years of its existence only inheritance could get you into the enclave; invited guests were allowed to stay no longer than two weeks. Members in-residence at their sprawling, 20-room "cottages" peaked during the January thru March period, cold months in northeastern states where most of these folks had permanent homes. When foreign warships appeared to be lurking about in its offshore waters in 1942, President Roosevelt ordered Jekyll evacuated. Its club never returned.

After World War II, the state of Georgia bought the island and made it into a state park. "Millionaire's Village" – a restored area on the western shore – hosts tours of the magnificent estates that the elite created as their playgrounds. You can also visit the site of Georgia's first brewery, which dates back to colonial times when the island grew hops and grains to make beer. A bridge now connects Jekyll to Brunswick, the largest city in the area. With four courses this vacationland is Georgia's largest golf resort. Tennis players can avail themselves of many facilities, including indoor courts built by J.P. Morgan which are now open to the public.

Sea Island, close neighbor to Jekyll, boasts the grandest hotel-vacation complex of all; the world-famous Cloister. At first the idea of Howard Coffin, who lived on Sapelo, to develop this strip of land – formerly called Long Island, Fifth Creek island, Isle of Palms, and Glynn Island – as a luxury resort, the island continues to thrive with well-appointed guest houses, newer condominiums, golf courses, and other recreational amenities. Coffin established an electric power plant and telephone system, as well as planning comfortably secluded, landscaped settings for up to three hundred large cottages and the grand, stuccoed, Spanish-style hotel itself. Finally, he constructed a causeway to bring guests over from the mainland and Sea, with its legendary Cloister, opened to a steady stream of famous visitors in 1928. The roster over the years includes Presidents Eisenhower, Coolidge, and Carter; Vice Presidents Alben Barkley and Hubert Humphrey; Governor Thomas E. Dewey; Queen Juliana of the Netherlands, and Winston Churchill, whose daughter, Sarah, was married on Sea Island. Those who loved it often returned for annual visits and sometimes to stay for good. The Georgia islands have always been popular retreats for writers, and the great American playwright Eugene O'Neill completed *Days Without End* and *Ah, Wilderness!* at "Casa Genotta," his beach house on Sea Island.

All this activity prompted a hastening in the residential development of St. Simons. Since Oglethorpe's tenure the adjacent island had been populated. After the battle of Bloody Marsh, remnants of a group of Salzburgers and some other settlers deserted the little town of Frederica for the mainland, but merchants soon moved in and made a central storage and trading business here, encouraging other areas of growth for the island. After the Revolutionary War the economic base changed to agriculture, with a number of successful plantation owners growing cotton and living the good life. However, not one of them ever owned or controlled St. Simons.

In the late eighteenth century, Major Pierce Butler brought a team of workers over from South Carolina to construct Hampton. This lay on the north end of the island, just across from Little St. Simons which he also owned. Over a dozen buildings eventually comprized his estate, including summerhouses, workshops, barns, stables, dairies, an imposing mansion and several other houses with formal gardens. Guests remembered the hospitality of the family and their neighbors, and the bounty of good food from the plantation. In 1839 Butler's son, Pierce II, and his wife, impetuous English actress Fanny Kemble, came over from their own rice plantation at Butler Island. Fanny recorded the experiences of her brief, unhappy Georgia sojourn in *Journal of a Residence on a Georgia Plantation*; a polemic against slavery in this land and full of rapturous praise for its natural beauty. Her work survives as one of the major accounts of American slave culture. The Butlers' daughters inherited Hampton and other properties. In 1900 a pencil manufacturer bought Little St. Simons, hoping to use its abundance of red cedar. However, the trees had grown so gnarled and crooked that they proved unsuitable, so the 12,000 acres remained a vacation retreat.

Island trees have long been felled for their choice lumber. In 1794, St. Simons produced live oak lumber for the U.S. frigate *Constitution*, which became famous as "Old Ironsides". Almost a hundred years later, the same prized timber was shipped north to help make the Brooklyn Bridge.

A lighthouse is, perhaps, the most prominent feature of any island. The U.S. government commissioned James Gould to build the first lighthouse on St. Simons in 1811 and appointed him keeper of the 75-foot structure. Confederate troops stationed here blew it up in 1862 to interrupt Union blockade runners off the coast. Charles B. Cluskey, the architect who did much work in Savannah, designed and constructed the present lighthouse on the same spot in 1872; the U.S. Coast Guard still maintains it.

Most of the rest of St. Simons past exists in ruins, remnants, and memories. What's left of Fort Frederica can be visited at the National Monument site. Ruins of a number of plantation buildings lie amid the present-day recreation areas and quiet neighborhoods. As St. Simons underwent gentle transformation into a twentieth-century, oceanside community, a number of historic and prehistoric sites were inadvertently located. Excavations around the airport revealed relics of an Indian village and burial ground, providing important information about ancient life here on the Georgia coast.

Inland from the Golden Isles the stories continue. Originally territory of the Creeks (one of the five civilized tribes), Guale, Yamasi and other Indian tribes, early Georgians built legendary rice plantations on the fertile ground, which was bisected by a series of rivers. The Civil War mutilated nearly all of these productive lands, and a way of life vanished along with the rice fields. Between Darien and Brunswick, one example of an antebellum property still exists. Hofwyl-Broadfield Plantation, owned by descendants of William Brailsford from 1806 to 1973, welcomes visitors to tour the 1850s house and grounds where rice was once cultivated. In its later years as an operating farm, Hofwyl-Broadfield converted to dairy production, demanding much less labor, and Guernsey and Jersey cattle grazed on marshlands and former rice fields. Other previous plantation estates have been taken over privately as recreational hunting retreats.

Much of the land in south Georgia is valued now for growing pine. A number of paper companies have field offices clustered around picturesque little towns like St. Marys – which claims to antedate St. Augustine, Florida, as the oldest city in the United States – and Folkston.

At Folkston you can enter one of the southeast's largest natural attractions; the Okefenokee Swamp. Elevated boardwalks and observation towers allow day visitors to safely observe the water fowl, alligators, snakes, other reptiles and creatures which inhabit ponds, streams, swamplands and forests. Adventuresome backpackers canoe deep into the swamp to camp and explore for weeks at a time. Mosquitoes have a permanent proprietary lease here; forewarned is forearmed.

The big city of Georgia's coastal region has always been Savannah. A few nearby barrier islands have a close historical association with it. But despite physiography, the cultural and social development of these islands long separated them from the Golden Isles. Today's visitor may be hardly aware of passing from one of these "suburban" islands to another, for they run together like pieces of a puzzle. Tybee Island, at the mouth of the Savannah River, developed into Savannah beach – the local resort connected to the city by a twenty-mile, palm tree-lined highway – now a run-down beach town trying to revive itself with time-share condominiums.

A hundred and fifty years ago, prominent Savannah families had gracious summer homes on Wilmington, Isle of Hope, and upon other pieces of solid ground laced by marshlands. Today's residents live year-round in quiet communities that coexist with the shrimp industry and a few other local enterprises. Part of Skidaway Island, and Wormsloe on Isle of Hope, have been set aside – after long years of protection as private properties – for marine research and as nature preserves.

The islands also served as a buffer for the city in time of war. Fort Jackson guarded Savannah from just before the War of 1812 until 1905. A team of engineers that included a young Robert E. Lee built Fort Pulaski between 1829 and 1847. Its massive brickwork walls crumpled under Union bombardment during the Civil War. Fort Screven, constructed on Tybee in 1875, was one of the last coastal fortifications. All three forts can be visited and have museums that chronicle chapters of military and coastal history.

Poets have immortalized the Golden Isles and their stories for centuries. Sitting under a giant oak near Brunswick, Sidney Lanier composed the most famous depiction, *The Marshes of Glynn*, which conveys the love and respect felt by all who come to know them.

She used to be called "the lady with a dirty face," and from her ubiquitous, powdery gray dirt to that persistent, permeating stench of Union Camp paper mill, Savannah could at best be described as a down-at-the-heels town that obviously must have enjoyed happier and more prosperous days. People who could afford it moved to new homes in the suburbs, America's symbol of affluence, and businesses fled a sagging economy, leaving behind a sad and tattered little outline of a compact city with nothing much – not even pride – to show the occasional visitor. Roughneck sailors frequented the Port Royal and a few other dingy bars along River Street. Not a stretch for an afternoon, much less a moonlight, stroll. Too many of the once-elegant homes around pocket-park squares suffered transition to weary and worn boarding houses, and the squares often dearly needed some tender loving care. Fire lanes had even been cut through some of them. Buildings were admired for their distinctive, mottled Savannah gray brick only to be dismantled piece by precious piece and carted off for some brand-new, split-level or ranch-style house miles away.

Vestiges of a prosperous century remained: isolated blocks on Oglethorpe Avenue, Charlton Street, Gaston and Jones Streets, seemed like a breath of fresh air. Broughton Street remained, as always, the main shopping thoroughfare. But by the early 1950s Savannah, taken as a whole, appeared hopelessly shabby; an embarrassing stepchild to the state whose roots lay here amid the remnants of glorious days. A rich and important history had been nearly buried by neglect and an apathy that grew from the distraction of other, more contemporary concerns. Only with the rose-colored glasses of imagination could one see any fulfillment of the original plan that its founder, James Edward Oglethorpe, had devised for Savannah in 1733.

General Oglethorpe had arrived with a hearty band of 114 English settlers and the design for the first town in a new colony. they selected a spot on Yamacraw Bluff about eighteen miles up to the Savannah River and there, following traditions that date back to ancient Roman military camps, set out a conservative grid area of lots and squares (always called squares, *never* referred to as parks), the first such planned community in the New World. Individual colonists received 50 acres of land, which included 60 x 90-foot plots in this inner area for houses; space for gardening and farming land lay beyond the core of city wards. Each ward contained forty tythings of ten house lots, planned symmetrically around a center square. Within two decades, Savannah had been developed following this pattern as far south as today's Oglethorpe Avenue, a dozen blocks from the river front, and to what is now Lincoln Street on the east and Jefferson Street on the west, an expanse of six blocks; the heart of a present-day historic district with six squares and a divided boulevard.

Most of the early structures were built of wood; timber – especially pine – being plentiful in this coastal region. As the name Savannah suggests, land here stretches out quite flat. So, even though a position away from the open sea provided shelter from the brunt of hurricanes and some other natural destructive forces, Savannah couldn't escape the devastation of fires which swept swiftly across the city more than once during her early history. Since the population had steadily increased to about 5,000 by the end of the century, they simply rebuilt, replacing the original 24 x 16-foot, one-story clapboard houses with sturdier structures. The character of a colonial settlement remained even though actual work by the first architects – including Colonel William Bull, Henry Flitcroft, William Gerar DeBrahm, Adrian Boucher, and a Mr. Day – is largely lost.

James Habersham's Pink House – a handsome stucco affair built in 1789 and sometimes referred to as the first brick building in Georgia – tenaciously survived some of those fires and lives on today as a gracious restaurant overlooking Reynolds Square. Among the extant architecture stands exemplary work by a bright young Englishman, William Jay. He arrived in Savannah in 1817 and proceeded to design and construct one of the finest English Regency houses in America. The Richardson-Owens-Thomas House, originally the home of Jay's brother-in-law, Richard Richardson, opened to the public as a museum in 1952. During his brief sojourn (he left for Charleston, South Carolina, in 1821 or 1822) this imaginative and gifted architect completed several other buildings of notable design. Those that survive are kept in good repair and welcome visitors to a glimpse of the elegant lifestyle which must have been enjoyed by the Richardsons, Scarboroughs, Telfairs and other first families of old Savannah.

Isaiah Davenport, a builder from Rhode Island, relocated at about the same time the young state began to flourish and develop its own style. He made himself a handsome home on Columbia Square (State and Habersham Streets) and, like William Jay, his work showed a penchant for graceful symmetry. This late Federal-style residence, built in 1821, features a double-staired, ornamental iron entry, interior columns separating the antehall from an elliptical staircase and matching columns adorning the drawing room. The Library of Congress holds original measured drawings for this outstanding example of early domestic architecture. But in 1955, following its decline into use as a multi-family dwelling, the former Davenport residence faced a wrecking ball, and the land was slated to become a parking lot.

Here begins the story of one of the most remarkable and successful urban preservation efforts. It not only physically transformed a city, but changed its self-image and the attitudes of its citizens. A small group of historically-minded residents had just lost a valiant fight to save Savannah's nineteenth-century City Market. The now-symbolic structure on Ellis Square (Barnard and Congress Streets – a traditional site for buying, selling, and trading goods) was razed and replaced by a utilitarian parking deck, hideously out of character with neighboring structures and the downtown area, but certainly reflecting the general American approval of progress and modernization at any cost. Determined that Savannah's heritage should not be sacrificed again, these devoted few, soon galvanized as the Historic Savannah Foundation, bought the Isaiah Davenport property to insure its preservation and found themselves on the threshold of a movement that transformed a shabby, depressed city into America's largest registered historic district – 3.3 miles within a National Landmark Historic District and the Victorian Historic District. The older area of Savannah has become one of the most pleasant and informative walking tours of any city. No formalities are necessary. Without even a guidebook – just general directions will do – one can set out to stroll at leisure into living history. For comfort's sake try to avoid the heat and humidity of summer. In fact, visit during early spring when virtually every plot of land blazes with brilliant fuchsias, purples, pinks, oranges, and reds of lush azaleas.

Many visitors have arrived at Savannah's Central of Georgia railroad terminal (designed and built by Augustus Schaab, 1860-1876) via the Nancy Hanks passenger train, which pulled in from Atlanta and points north at about midnight. The Nancy runs no more, but the Central of Georgia building on West Broad Street, made from famous Savannah gray brick and featuring some marvelous arched bridges, has a new dual life as Visitors Center and Chamber of Commerce, so it's still the place to begin your sojourn. By all means leave your car in their ample parking lot. You can't possibly enjoy this historical community encumbered by an anomalous modern invention. Pick up a good map and whatever brochures they are offering and head north, toward the river, on West Broad.

In a few blocks you will come to an imposing Greek Revival building, the William Scarborough House. It was built to a William Jay design, has been splendidly restored and is now the headquarters for the Historic Savannah Foundation. Scarborough, a financier and cotton merchant, commissioned a Regency-style mansion in 1818, intended to be the most lavish residence of its day in Savannah. Jay completed it just in time to entertain President James Monroe when he visited the city to celebrate the transatlantic steamship *S.S. Savannah's* maiden voyage. Scarborough invested heavily in this venture which soon failed, ultimately losing him most of his fortune, including the West Broad mansion. Then, for ninety years, the building housed a public school for black students in the neighborhood.

When the Historic Savannah Foundation eventually bought it, the three-story structure had crumbled to an uninhabitable slum. Not only did these preservationists restore the notable home to its former glory – with a fan window at the entrance, formal drawing rooms, columned interiors, center atrium reaching three stories up to a blue arched ceiling and skylight – but they have set up their headquarters here where they sometimes sponsor expertly-presented exhibitions and lectures on the historical restoration of early Americana. Their model role in urban preservation included a revolving fund for purchasing historic or aesthetically important buildings threatened with demolition that can then be resold to private restorers. The Foundation concerns itself with overseeing Savannah's architectural heritage and city plan in the two registered historic districts and offers advice, guidance, and certain resources to individuals involved in the actual restoration projects. Although they failed in their very first preservation attempt to save the old

City Market, the organization salvaged some pieces of it and now plans to incorporate these remnants into a new structure on the original site, ironically razing the Park 'n' Shop garage which replaced the old marketplace. All about the city you will notice the influence that the Historic Savannah Foundation continues to have; they claim responsibility for saving over 1,000 buildings.

Leaving the Scarborough House, walk around the corner to Montgomery and Bryan Streets and visit First Bryan Baptist Church. John B. Hogg, Savannah's city engineer, designed the building (constructed 1873-1888) and church members came from the oldest black congregation in the U.S. Head east and then north around Ellis Square and that horrid but symbolic parking garage, up a few short blocks to a park-like aisle along the bluff known as Factor's Walk. The system of iron bridges and factors' buildings date back to the nineteenth century when cotton was king and this area hummed with all the activities that made it Savannah's economic center. Pause next to City Hall at Oglethorpe's bench, commemorating the spot he pitched his tent on February 12, 1733 (an event Savannah celebrates for a week each year), before descending the steep stone stairs or cobblestone street down to the river front. All of the city's cobblestones originally served as ballast on English merchant ships that then left the port laden with cotton bales.

River Street, only quite recently scruffy, dingy and assiduously avoided by most folks, attracts tourists and natives to its lively row of shops and restaurants. The one new structure here at the western edge of this revitalized commercial strip sticks out literally and figuratively and detracts from an otherwise well-scaled, coordinated, and open public district. It's puzzling why this Hyatt Hotel, in such a prize location, features utilitarian institutional design, clashing wildly with its neighbors. For a different perspective on the architecture of the Factor's Walk area, take Cap'n Sam's boat tour up and down the river. You'll get a close up of the industrious, little red tugboats and the other activity in the nation's tenth busiest port. The buildings rise abruptly five to six stories measured from the river. Because of the bluff on the Bay Street side, which they face, the height appears to be only two or three stories (uniform with most of the city-scape). Notice the iron balconies on the back of these former counting rooms and warehouses, complementing the ironwork bridges connecting them at street level on the front. Charles B. Cluskey, an Irish architect whose mid-nineteenth-century work in Savannah is considered second in importance and influence only to Jay's, designed much of this area.

Only two, maybe three, of the River Street tenants have been around for any length of time. A tidied-up Port Royal continues (with more genteel patrons, too) and the Boar's Head Restaurant still offers elegant meals with a front-row view of the river. Of course, most harbors have their legendary figures remembered in lore or more formally. From 1887-1931 the familiar figure of Florence Martus, a woman from nearby Elba Island, faithfully stood watch on the banks and saluted river traffic, using a handkerchief by day and a lantern by night. A bronze statue of the Waving Girl with her dog recalls that "her immortality stems from her friendly greeting to passing ships. A welcome to strangers entering the port and a farewell to wave them safely onward."

One other monument stands above in the row facing Bay Street – the lovely red brick Cotton Exchange (1886 by William G. Preston), a gentle reminder of times past. Just in front of its companion, lion fountain, pause to read the historical marker commemorating a 1785 charter of America's first state university. It's a first also claimed by neighboring North Carolina. Walk down to the end of adjacent Emmet Park where Bay Street meets East Broad.

When the English trustees drew up plans for the new colony they included provision for what amounted to an experimental agricultural station. In 1734 settlers established Trustees' Garden – sometime name of the general area – just west of this present-day intersection. Someone had the grand idea to plant mulberry trees in hopes of rivalling China as a silk-producer. Wrong! They enjoyed better luck with spices and tropical fruit. The garden, situated strategically above the river approach to the city, soon found itself doing duty as a fort anyway.

After the British occupation (1778-1782) the fort was officially named Fort Wayne for General "Mad Anthony" Wayne. The federal government later took claim of the site and constructed a heavy-duty brick fortress. After the War of 1812, with the population increasing, the area was turned over for residential use, and in 1848 Savannah Gas Company purchased the property. By 1945 the housing here had deteriorated to slums remembered as the worst in Savannah. The wife of the gas company president, a woman with extraordinary vision, decided that this historic plot and its dilapidated structures could and should be rehabilitated. Photographs taken before reconstruction show rubble and weeds, and neglected buildings collapsing from disrepair. East Broad was beset with a horrid reputation at this time and author Richard Jessup, himself a native Savannahian, set his tragic novel *The Damned don't Cry* here. With a lot of determination and hard work this first major restoration and revitalization project in Savannah got underway – it antedated Historic Savannah Foundation by ten years although it wasn't completed until 1961 – and importantly gave life back to the fort section, setting a precedent for saving this historic city.

Now people come here from all over the world to dine at the famous Pirate's House. With its genuine weather-beaten exteriors, the restaurant – actually a cluster of small frame buildings – has been decorated with gaslights, red-checked tablecloths, and fishermen's nets, and boasts legends and ghosts of Jolly Roger and his less jovial compatriots. Menus are gargantuan and thematically cute. You can't get away with less than a generous meal, so walk it off in a tour around Trustees' Garden – lovely even after dark when a plethora of gaslights flicker over delicate flowerbeds and the architecturally diverse village.

Traveling west for a few blocks on St. Julian Street one passes a multi-hued mix of eighteenth and nineteenth-century frame houses set off by tiny manicured gardens. Local lore says that a ghost still haunts number 507, a handsomely restored three-story clapboard also known for a distinctive widow's walk perched atop it. From these quiet residential blocks around Washington and Warren Squares, St. Julian skirts Reynolds and Johnson Squares where John Wesley, among others, made much history. A recently sculpted likeness of Reverend Wesley presides over Reynolds Square and the hotel bearing his name stands on the site of Georgia's first church, next door to the Oliver Sturges House (1813) where William Scarborough and others made some of their plans for the *S.S. Savannah*, and just across from James Habersham's unmistakable Pink House. The Sturges House is now a working example of a restored historical building comfortably accommodating private business offices.

Charles and John Wesley, well-known as founders of Methodism, sailed from England in 1736 aboard ship with a band of Moravians also destined for Georgia. Charles traveled on to minister at St. Simon's Island for what turned out to be a brief and not very happy time. John remained in Savannah where the colony's parish had been established upon the arrival of the first settlers in 1733. Savannahians proudly recount "firsts" for which Wesley was responsible: the oldest Sunday School in America, founded at Christ Church in 1736, the first English hymnal published in America, 1737. Perhaps he was also the first clergyman to leave the colony in public disgrace. The young woman of whom he was enamored, Sophie Hopkey, eloped with another man. Wesley thereafter denied her communion, and her family brought a legal suit which resulted in a magistral order that he not leave the colony. However, after one year and nine months of preaching the gospel "not as I ought, but as I was able," Wesley returned to England amid the great evangelical movement that gave birth to the Methodist Church. Savannah Methodists later designated Wesley Monumental Church in recognition of his leadership in the movement.

Christ Church on Johnson Square stands on part of the plot originally appointed by Oglethorpe for its establishment. The building has been replaced several times, the present one dating from 1838 with an interior reconstructed in 1897. James Hamilton Couper designed this outstanding example of Greek Revival architecture which has simple features not unlike an ancient temple. The church, as so many Savannah houses of worship, keeps its doors unlocked in the daytime and welcomes visitors for a quiet respite. A monument in the handsome, shady square which it faces marks the grave of Revolutionary War hero General Nathanael Greene. Morrison's Cafeteria, a different sort of landmark on the other side of the square, serves simple home-style southern food all day long. Sip a glass of iced tea at a window seat and watch the world saunter by. Notice that the red brick wall across the way tastefully conceals a parking deck; its twentieth-century design graciously accommodating a much older setting. Over in the other direction Savannah Bank and Trust put up the city's only skyscraper – reaching only fifteen stories – in 1911.

Here at Johnson Square begins one of the loveliest stretches of the walking tour. Wear your most comfortable shoes and bring along a camera or photographic memory. The squares along the way have plenty of benches if you need a rest or just want to stop and savor the surroundings. Col. William Bull came over from South Carolina to assist Oglethorpe in 1733. They named a street in his honor; it runs north-south starting at City Hall (1905) on Bay Street and looping around five squares (Johnson Square being first) and Forsyth Park.

Chief Tomochichi, indispensable ally to the colonists, had been curiously ostracized by the Creek Indians. He and his small band of outcast Yamacraws greeted the arriving white men, helped them clear land, build, plant, and served as a buffer against less friendly tribes. Oglethorpe even invited Tomochichi and a few others along on a much-publicized 1734 visit to King George II of England. They obligingly paraded about royal courts in native costume, sat for portraits, shared tobacco and other American products. The venerable Tomochichi died at age 97 and lies buried in Wright Square under the center monument to William Washington Gordon (founder of the Central of Georgia railroad and father of Juliet Gordon Low) and not beneath a large boulder in the southeast corner which commemorates his own contributions.

Even if you've never participated in the annual spring Girl Scout cookie rite, stop in to see their National Center at the intersection of Bull Street and Oglethorpe Avenue. Founder Juliet Gordon Low grew up in this 1820 house, which has been restored and furnished with pieces from 1860-1880, many of them belonging to the Gordon family. William Jay may have designed this building – Savannah's first Registered National Landmark – and, if so, a total of four examples of his work remain extant in this city. Later the Gordon House was enlarged by Detlef Lienau. Troops of Brownies and Girl Scouts from all over the world come every year, especially around March 12, the date in 1912 that Mrs. Low convened her first troop meeting at an Abercorn Street carriage house.

Diagonally across Bull Street from this pale pink Regency home stands Independent Presbyterian Church, whose congregation dates itself back to 1755. The present stark gray stone and slate building had to be reconstructed in 1891 from plans for the 1817 church that was destroyed by fire. Historical markers point out that Woodrow Wilson married Ellen Axson in the old manse here in 1885. Savannahians do like recalling visits of American presidents to their fair city. Bostonian Lowell Mason, the great music educator and composer of hymns, served as Independent's organist in the early nineteenth century.

Chippewa Square honors James Edward Oglethorpe

with a bronze statue. The First Baptist Church, another Greek temple-styled edifice, claims to be Savannah's oldest standing house of worship. Elias Carter made the original design in 1833. Charles Cluskey is probably responsible for the porticoed mansion at the corner of McDonough Street, with a third floor added some sixty or seventy years after its 1844 construction. William Jay built a theater on this square, the site of a more modern theater in operation today. A little two-story clapboard house at the corner of Perry Street dates back to 1820 and has stood there unchanged with all the other architectural changes taking place around it.

Liberty Street, the next main east-west thoroughfare, used to be the address of Savannah's grandly ornate Victorian hotel, the DeSoto – a funny old red and green hulk tastefully replaced in the 1960s with a more graceful and modern brick DeSoto Hilton. Too bad the original swimming pool couldn't be saved for, with its surrounding tropical garden, it was one of the finest hotel pools anywhere. For visitors seeking older and more intimate accommodation, the neighborhood has a few bed and breakfast establishments or small inns.

Another famous Charles Cluskey house, known as the Sorrel-Weed, built in 1841, faces Madison Square opposite the rear of the DeSoto. The Meldrim-Green House, by John S. Norris, another well-known architect who worked here, overlooks the square from the west. This prime example of Gothic Revival inadvertently played host to the most unwelcome guest in the city's history; General William T. Sherman completed his march to the sea at Savannah in 1864. Cotton merchant Charles Green, who had commissioned the house, offered it to Sherman for use as his personal headquarters in exchange for his promise to spare the city. The scheme worked and today the iron-trimmed, dark brick mansion serves adjacent St. John's Episcopal Church as its parish house.

Bull Street's last square perhaps graces it the most elegantly. A center monument remembers Count Casimir Pulaski, who lost his life in the Siege of Savannah (1779). Houses (all private) on surrounding Bull, Taylor, and Gordon Streets display some of the city's finest and most unusual ornamental ironwork. John Norris constructed 429 Bull, ancestral home of American lyricist Johnny Mercer, in 1860. The imposing, Italianate design features an ornamented overhanging roof, elaborate balconies and windows of cast iron. Next to this freestanding mansion you pass Savannah's most outstanding English row houses, built in 1858. The twin four-story stucco structures show off cast iron entrance porticoes with covered balconies. Lacy ironwork fences in surrounding gardens. Historic Hebrew Congregation Mickve Israel (1876-78) faces the square from the opposite side. Among the earliest colonists to arrive after Oglethorpe, its roots go back to 1734. Many of the elegant buildings between here and Gaston Street at the head of Forsyth Park, despite their residential appearances, have served institutional purposes, mostly for Armstrong College before it relocated to the suburbs. Now behind the quiet, restored facades you will find law offices or antique dealers and designers conducting business.

Forsyth Park, known to some children as "the big park," functions as an urban green space with something for everyone: fully-equipped playgrounds, tennis courts, a fragrance garden for the blind, plenty of benches – for weary tourists and other people-watchers – along wide promenades, and a graceful fountain at the center. The azaleas here, blossoming anytime from mid-February, make the most beautiful display of color in the city. Great trees stand graciously festooned with Spanish moss. Find the local peanut vendor – he's usually stationed near the fountain – and please share your cache with the inveterate park denizens: friendly squirrels and pigeons.

Forsyth technically and stylistically lies in the Victorian District. If you venture onto Huntingdon, Hall, or Gwinnett Streets, or further south along Park and Duffy, you'll see blocks of spruced up Victorian gingerbreads; old homes by American standards, yet younger than those in the heart of Savannah.

Serious history buffs should visit Hodgson Hall (1876 by Detlef Lienau), library of the Georgia Historical Society at the corner of the park (Gaston and Whitaker Streets). Over 30,000 volumes – books, manuscripts, maps, photographs, and other documents – that pertain to the history of the state and region have been collected and cataloged. Notable historians have served as curators and directors of the Society.

Continue your walking tour north on Whitaker. A remarkable row of houses extends across the foot of Chatham Square and beyond. Fifteen houses called Gordon Row were constructed in a single unit in 1853. Typically, the four-story main buildings feature high stoops with ornamental iron stairways. On the lane behind stretches a matching block-long row of carriage houses. A few steps north and west, at Jones and Jefferson Streets, you may meet the locals at their neighborhood joint, the Crystal Beer Parlor. In fact, as this area changed from bad to worse and then underwent its renaissance, the Crystal stayed right there – serving great hamburgers of ground-on-the-premises beef, huge onion rings dipped in a homemade batter, thick-cut potatoes, and oversized drinks – in simple, nearly drab, surroundings.

Residential Jones Street, most of it distinctively paved in red brick, merits an attentive stroll from one end to the other. Some owners keep apartments or rooms for overnight guests; watch for discreet signs if you're interested. Typical nineteenth-century Savannah domestic architecture shows an English influence. Houses usually of the three-bay width rise two stories over a basement level and feature a high, covered stoop. Owners usually hang out plaques denoting provenance of each dwelling and, for the most part, their historical data is accurate.

If you wish to experience the ultimate southern dinner (an everyday noontime meal) served in authentic regional style, wait in the lane that wends its way down the sidewalk from 107 West Jones. Mrs. Wilkes continues to receive accolades from all over the world for her home cooking – greens, black-eyed peas, rice and gravy, fried chicken, ham, biscuits, cornbread, etc. – laid out on groaning tables where patrons, seated family-style, pass platters and help themselves to all they can eat for a bargain price. It's a Savannah institution.

A good place to head north again is at Habersham Street, then turning west onto Charlton at the foot of Troup Square. Flannery O'Connor, who lived most of her life near Milledgeville in middle Georgia, was born at 207 East Charlton, a narrow little house built in 1856. Most of the houses in this block and nearby blocks on Harris, Liberty and, of course, East Jones Streets, date from mid to late nineteenth century.

Cotton broker Andrew Low had Charles Cluskey build him a residence at Charlton and Abercorn Streets in 1847. Now maintained by the National Society of the Colonial Dames of America, who make it their state headquarters, it had Juliet Gordon Low as its mistress following her marriage to Andrew's son William. (The rear carriage house served as that famous first Girl Scout meeting place.) Distinguished guests have included English writer William Makepeace Thackeray and General Robert E. Lee. An ironwork balcony extends across the facade before four symmetrically-placed, full-length shuttered windows.

Abercorn Street, another grand north-south walk, loops around Lafayette Square. The Cathedral of St. John the Baptist dates back to 1876 and here, traditionally, the annual St. Patrick's Day parade, one of the nation's largest, starts off. It ends at Emmet Park (named for Irish patriot Robert Emmet) overlooking the river near traditional Irish neighborhoods. During the colonial period Savannah did not admit Catholics, fearing a possible allegiance of such settlers to the Spanish; today it is the largest diocese south of Washington D.C.

Just ahead on Abercorn (entrance on Oglethorpe Avenue) colonists established Georgia's first cemetery, until 1895 affiliated with Christ Church. Some early citizens of the city lie buried here, including well-known civic and military leaders. A large, white marble monument marks the supposed grave of Button Gwinnett, one of Georgia's three signers of the Declaration of Independence. Colonial Park Cemetery, now cared for by the municipal government, marks the city's original lower boundary.

This stretch of Oglethorpe Avenue boasts some of Savannah's proudest and most historic structures. The little house at 122 East Oglethorpe, built for Christian Camphor in 1760-67, may be the oldest building in Georgia. Originally a one-story cottage, the brick base added in 1871 raised it to two levels. Many of the eighteenth-century houses in these blocks underwent exterior alterations in subsequent centuries: removal or addition of balconies, porches, enlargements, new wings, etc. One of Historic Savannah Foundations's earliest and most dramatic preservation projects saved Mary Marshall Row (numbers 230-244). They purchased the 1855 four-story pairs of brick houses for $9,000 in 1959, just in time to keep them from a wrecker's ball. America's man of letters and Pulitzer Prize winner Conrad Aiken lived at number 230. All houses here remain private.

North just a few blocks on Columbia Square you can visit Isaiah Davenport's restored 1815 house furnished finely with family heirlooms and other treasures of the Georgian period. Loop east to Greene Square and notice smaller, plainer buildings of the same period. To the west on Oglethorpe Square stands another monumental architectural gem. Allow time for a leisurely tour of the Richardson-Owens-Thomas House. In the formal dining room, to the left as you enter, observe William Jay's obsession with detail and symmetry in his designs. To complete an interior oval he used curved corner doors, including one that is false. He selected decorative amber glass so that even on a rainy day bright light would shine in the room. Museum guides will give you a thorough tour and point out features of the house that make it an important case study for architectural historians. They will undoubtedly tell you that the Marquis de Lafayette made a speech from the little balcony facing York Street. Take a walk in the formal garden behind the house and don't miss seeing the kitchen on the basement level, a remarkable collection of nineteenth-century utensils and equipment in a facility used for cooking, baking and other food preparation and storage.

Head west to Wright Square (Bull and State Streets), site of a fine public building erected in 1895 and finished under supervision of architect William Martin Aiken in 1898. The massive white Georgia marble edifice, built to serve as a post office, fits among smaller scaled structures because of its delicate ornamentation and the ingenious use of loggias at various levels. Complementary Spanish, French, and Italian elements blend well in the overall scheme.

One square over, Telfair at Barnard Street, another William Jay mansion, known as Telfair Academy of Arts and Sciences, opened as the south's first public art museum in 1886. Originally home of Alexander Telfair – son of an early Georgia governor – his family occupied it from 1820 until they bequeathed it for its present purpose. By policy, works of living artists are not exhibited. In addition to impressionist paintings and a collection of etchings, some rooms contain period furniture and display silver and china. The Academy occasionally sponsors concerts and lectures. The mother church of Georgia Methodism, Trinity Church, stands next door. John B. Hogg designed the building in 1848.

A short walk south on Barnard Street to Orleans Square brings you to Savannah's twentieth-century Civic Center, an auditorium and convention hall. Aaron Champion's columned 1844 house, with an overgrown front garden, faces it. Except for a third floor added in 1895 the architecture is attributed to Charles Cluskey.

You've toured through 250 years of living history in a remarkably compact urban area. Savannah's treasure trove of historical and architectural gems, valiantly rescued for posterity, remain lived in, cared for, and lovingly preserved. She's a city with a beautiful face, scrubbed clean and wearing a bright smile.

Those of us who first knew Atlanta in the 1950s look at it now with mixed feelings of familiarity and strangeness. Too many of the friendly old landmarks have vanished over the decades, except in our memories. Other places we remember hang on tenaciously and some have withstood time only to be altered, transformed, brought up-to-date. Much of what does remain looks funny and uncomfortable in its new setting; anachronisms created by progress. Newer, bigger, better, faster – all desirable in the changing life of this city concerned above everything else with progressing. Before this bold, aggressive spirit of self-advancement caught Atlanta and whisked it onto a new whirlwind course of growth, the little city in Georgia's piedmont seemed indistinguishable from many of the other southern capitals.

Trolley lines powered by overhead current ran out ten miles or so to suburbs – smaller towns like Avondale, Decatur, Hapeville. People could come into the city to work or shop and catch the last trolley home by eight in the evening. Often as not those bulky old streetcars would jump their connections and strand passengers mid-trip until the transit authority's repair service could be roused for a road call.

The Atlanta airport consisted of a drafty, makeshift concourse – a temporary wooden affair, like a long, dim, musty hallway. It looked like army surplus and probably was. Most folks took the train anyway – out of Union Station if they were headed north or Terminal Station for southerly destinations.

The palatial Fox Theater – modeled on an Egyptian mosque, with turrets, domes and a ceiling made to look like a summer night's sky of twinkly stars and clouds that floated about, as well as a mighty Wurlitzer organ – showed first-run movies except when the touring Metropolitan Opera moved in for a week each May as they had annually since 1912. The Municipal Auditorium, a concrete barn, hosted just about everybody else who came to town, like Holiday on Ice, theatrical touring companies and musical acts, wrestling matches, livestock shows, state education conventions and local high school graduations or an occasional concert by the Atlanta Symphony Orchestra under its conductor Henry Sopkin.

Georgia Tech Yellow Jackets challenged football teams from Auburn, Clemson, and other schools around the southeast on perfect, crisp, autumn Saturday afternoons at Grant Field. The traditional match against the Georgia Bulldogs from Athens came at the end of the college season, after the Baby 'dogs and Jackets (freshmen of the gridiron set) clashed on Thanksgiving Day. In the stickyl hot, summertime minor league Atlanta Crackers lined up against other AA baseball clubs, like Birmingham and Chattanooga at Cracker Stadium out on Ponce de Leon across from the big Sears & Roebuck store.

Sears could be good for some fun on a Saturday outing, and you had a choice of shopping in the retail store or going up and ordering from the catalog department. For most people serious shopping meant Rich's or Davison's – no branches, just big downtown department stores that always had entertaining window displays and helpful sales women who called you "honey" or "sugar." Or you might go to specialty shops like Muse's, J.P. Allen, Regenstein's where the clerks would know your name, your size and your color preference. Weary shoppers stopped at S & W Cafeteria on Peachtree (where else!). Ladies in pastel uniforms adorned with crisply starched handkerchiefs served meals all day long. The iced tea (refills on the house) came already sweetened, and they baked the most memorable blueberry muffins and bran muffins.

The tallest building downtown stood fifteen – maybe twenty – stories. The area never made much sense. Buildings didn't lie cheek-by-jowl; even then parking lots interrupted the streetscape, and landmarks always seemed scrambled around. No street ran parallel to any other and, with the exception of Peachtree, people had a hard time keeping street names of the inner city straight. Small wonder the main intersection came to be known as Five Points. At least the maze of railroad tracks had been tucked away under a system of viaducts.

Nobody lived downtown. Nobody had for a long time. A few central hotels like the Dinkler and the Biltmore took care of out-of-town visitors, who were mostly traveling businessmen. Old close-in neighborhoods, like West End and Grant Park, started to fade and lose their comfortable, stable appeal. An exodus of established families from Inman Park, billed years before as Atlanta's first suburb, had already begun. As people moved on to newer suburban developments in Fulton and DeKalb, Atlanta's two counties, older housing they left behind fell into disrepair and neglect.

The population increased at the same time it retreated from the city's core. Atlanta's municipal government gave chase in some directions and annexed communities such as Buckhead, about six miles to the northeast, early on in the '50s suburban land rush. Sometimes, though, they just couldn't keep up. After all, the postwar baby boom had hit town.

Everywhere we could see the evidence. Overcrowded elementary schools in DeKalb operated two sessions a day for several years until enough new buildings could be constructed. First graders, who had eagerly anticipated reading Dick and Jane primers in the neighborhood schoolhouse, instead got bussed off to temporary quarters in a church building. New subdivisions of split-level and ranch-style houses on cul-de-sacs – called Terraces, Courts, Places in modern real estate argot – were eclipsed by still newer housing developments before the ink dried on the blueprints. By the time we reached high school the doubling up process seemed a normal part of our education.

Business followed the migrating population. Neighborhood shopping centers replaced small working farms, some that had hung on even within the city limits. All this growth had been so unplanned that often a patch of woods or a horse pasture remained, juxtaposed to a brand-new apartment complex or shopping area. These little pockets of nature, in plain view of the city's now-expanding skyline, supplemented children's playgrounds as places to explore after school and in the summertime.

Driving over two-lane country roads from one part of Atlanta's environs to another, we could watch the dairy farms sprawled across green rolling hills sell out one by one to urbanization. Witnessing the symbolic passing of a quieter era tempered excitement over representative leaps forward. Next the cement mixers and bulldozers came out in full force to fell trees and pave a six-lane thoroughfare along the country roadbed. Scenes often repeated.

We forgot to look back and imagine Atlanta when she rose, like the phoenix of the city seal, from the ashes after Sherman's infamous Civil War burning. In the late nineteenth century, planners – such as famous landscape architect Frederick Law Olmsted and local businessman and engineer Joel Hurt – laid out open public spaces and neighborhoods of special character in a hilly terrain graced by natural woodlands. Great oaks formed soaring, natural archways across Lullwater, Oakdale and other streets in the Druid Hills section, which Olmsted and others laid out in 1908. The houses here sat back from the road at various levels. Streets climbed hills, wound across creeks, skirted a golf course and Fernbank Forest. Even though Druid Hills stood as an outstanding example of suburban planning and had been widely and consistently recognized as a desirable place to live – gracious and distinctive homes that didn't disturb the natural setting – new developers ignored conservative ideas. At this time anything old was something to be forgotten.

So who can remember what occupied a great tract of

land located on the north side now known as Lenox Square. Retailing met suburban Atlantans on their own turf and the floodgates opened. Lenox premiered in the late 1950s as the southeast's largest shopping center. Thousands and thousands of people could park their cars on an asphalt sea and shop two levels of major department stores, smaller boutiques, supermarkets, have dinner at any of several restaurants, go to a movie...it had everything until, in a few years, it was no longer big enough or modern enough to accommodate all the merchants who wanted to be there. Eventually new wings went out in every direction, they put a roof over it all and made it air conditioned. The granddaddy of Atlanta's retailing complexes (in less than twenty years!) set the precedent for large, comfortable malls to spring up in every affluent community around town.

Atlanta, by the early '60s, meant a five-county metropolitan area. The city met with resistance when it sought to officially absorb adjacent unincorporated communities. So to reach the population goal of one million, the growing cluster of suburbs got a new umbrella identification – Greater Atlanta. Many of the towns inside these boundaries – Lithonia, Doraville, Decatur, Marietta – predated Atlanta which wasn't founded until 1837. Each had a post office, a main street, a little business district, a few old-timers, and its own special character until the encroachment of real estate developers with their cookie cutter plans. They laid out tract after similar tract of bedroom communities and chipped away at long-standing individual identity.

The inevitable freeway system, built mostly during the 1960s, linked everything. Citizens watched its spokes slice right through old neighborhoods, plowing away hundreds of houses but making automobile transportation to and from outlying communities convenient. Soon it seemed you couldn't get anywhere without at least one freeway exit per set of directions. Public transportation limped along, largely inadequate and unused (unusable!) by most commuters, even though the trolleys had long since been dismantled and replaced by orange City Slicker buses.

Atlanta wanted desperately to be the New York of the South, a qualitative and quantitative comparison which had been applied off and on for nearly a hundred years. Obviously the compactness that makes New York and other large cities so dense and overwhelming had escaped city planners in this part of Georgia. Downtown lost its compelling appeal, if indeed it ever had any. You could reside in the suburbs and shop in the suburbs and be entertained in the suburbs, so why shouldn't you work there too? Freeways gave birth to office parks. Clusters of multi-storied buildings surrounded by lawns and trees mushroomed conveniently near off-ramps all around the metropolitan area. Now you could live here and be identified with a city yet have little need ever to visit a congested area with sidewalks and tall buildings.

Downtown fought the loss and diffusion of some of its resources by its own building activity. For all the strength – economic, political, and demographic – that spread farther and farther away, downtown remained at least a symbol of Atlanta's emergence as a major city of the new south. The first skyscraper to top twenty-five floors went up in the early 1950s – a red brick Fulton National Bank appropriately in front of a statue honoring Henry W. Grady, prominent Atlanta journalist and editor who first spoke of the new south in the late nineteenth century. The race upward was on. Next the Bank of Georgia two blocks away rose thirty-odd stories and installed the Top of Peachtree Restaurant, where businessmen and ladies' luncheon groups got a meal with a view in the direction of their choosing. In a few years, by the late 1960s, First National Bank across the street erected its forty-one floor tower.

About this time a young architect named John Portman, a local boy who had graduated from Georgia Tech, started to change the skyline on Peachtree a few blocks north. In the process he also defined contemporary American hotel architecture and made a considerable impact on the future of development in inner cities. Portman's first projects included a large, chunky Merchandise Mart (since expanded and now one of the biggest such marts in the country) and his prototypical Hyatt Regency. With its atrium rising the entire twenty-three story height of the structure, interior glass bubble elevators, a balconied facade and blue-domed revolving restaurant, the hotel became a major attraction even before it was completed.

Portman announced his plans for a whole complex city-within-a-city in this area of Peachtree, called Peachtree Center (what else!). The Mart, a neighboring tower, the Hyatt, a pair of office towers across the street with a vertical shopping mall and outdoor cafe and garden became its core, all connected above street-level by pedestrian bridges. The architect redesigned the ratty old Trailways Bus Station and linked it with a bridge too. He revealed his capstone in all this urban revitalization – a seventy-one story hotel, billed as the world's tallest, to be raised at the highest point on Peachtree Street. A dark, sleek, cylindrical figure, the Peachtree Plaza features, of course, an atrium (seven floors high), glass elevators sliding up (on the exterior this time) to a revolving restaurant, indoor fountains, waterfalls and a concrete pond.

Downtown Atlanta started to gear itself toward the visitor, particularly the convention visitor. The old Municipal Auditorium had been an embarrassment long enough, so the city cleared an area of run-down housing called Buttermilk Bottoms and built itself a new yellow brick auditorium – appointed with brilliant red carpeting throughout and lit by sparkling chandeliers – with an adjacent matching exhibit hall. It could host several thousand people comfortably. Other hotels and motels sprang up in the immediate vicinity. If activity here weren't enough, on the southwest of downtown the giant Omni got underway: hotel, ice rink, shops, and restaurants all under one massive roof with an indoor arena next door. Soon the Georgia World Congress Center would break ground on the same block. Atlanta looked like one big construction zone.

If the big time had arrived, then the city needed to prove that status. In the name of urban renewal another section of substandard housing, just south of the central business district, the state capitol and offices (the latter mostly stunning white Georgia marble edifices) was cleared for a major league stadium. In 1965 the National League's Milwaukee Braves moved in as did a new football franchise, the Falcons. People forgot all about a few summers before when the Atlanta Crackers, by then an AAA club, had led the International League in the standings all season. Now we had Phil Niekro and Felipe Alou and the great Hank Aaron, who hammered home run number 715 out of Atlanta-Fulton County Stadium in April 1974, breaking Babe Ruth's previous all-time record.

Perhaps it summed up Atlanta's spirit; a striving to overachieve, to overshadow past accomplishments. The city competed in all fields. A few miles north on the long-time site of the High Museum of Art, a coalition of arts groups erected and dedicated their $13 million multi-purpose culture palace in 1968. The Robert W. Woodruff Arts Center houses rehearsal and performance facilities for the Atlanta Symphony Orchestra, Alliance Theater, Atlanta Children's Theater; also the Atlanta College of Art and the High Museum remained on the premises. The Orchestra went out and hired for itself well-known conductor Robert Shaw, replaced much of the string section with talented young musicians fresh out of conservatories, made itself a full-time working organization and a musical group to be contended with. The Alliance developed into a first-rate regional theater company relying on considerable home-grown talent. In addition to their regular series for the adults, these two groups and the Atlanta Children's Theater invite Atlanta schoolchildren to special performances in their respective Arts Center halls, and they tour the southeast, taking Bach, Brahms, Berlioz, Shakespeare, and Tennessee Williams to the hinterlands. The best of New York comes down every year to work with them in Atlanta; a source of great local pride.

The High Museum finally outgrew its Arts Center quarters and in 1983 moved next door, to a pristine, sleek new $20 million home designed by architect Richard Meier. This part of town – north of Tenth Street along Peachtree and West Peachtree Streets – has always been the artsy community. Local galleries – some old standbys of twenty years or more – exhibit and sell photography, pottery, paintings, and sculpture of Georgia artists. Smaller dance and theater companies have organized all over the city producing and presenting an array of talent and much industrious work. The participants tend to be young, fiercely dedicated, and openly supportive of each other. Without a doubt the arts activity and standards of Atlanta influence and set an example for the entire region.

An Atlanta tradition takes place every spring in Piedmont Park. Frederick Law Olmsted designed Piedmont, on land which had been a farm, in 1887 for the Piedmont Exposition. It covers 185 acres, and the city bought it in 1904 for $93,000. Piedmont withstood all the years of change. First there was a succession of state fairs. Then it gradually filled up with golfers, boaters, swimmers, picnickers, and ball players. But there came a time when people ignored convenient urban recreation facilities for newly-popular weekend drives to northeast Georgia lakes and suburban country clubs. In all fairness, too, the Parks Department hadn't taken very good care of the properties. So the hippies moved into Piedmont during their heyday of peace, love and drugs in the '60s. The park emerged abused, but new public interest helped get it tidied up, and Atlanta folks go there once again. Even during its dreariest years, however, the Piedmont Arts Festival came to the park every spring and took over pavilions, gazebos, and bandstands, put up tents and stalls, and invited artists came to show and sell their work. Local musicians, dancers, mimes, and puppeteers entertained. Everyone else followed with kids and dogs and picnic baskets. For over thirty years Atlanta has been celebrating itself at the Arts Festival which usually runs for at least ten days in May.

Most of the civic celebrations here do take place in the springtime. Atlanta's dogwood blossom is like nowhere else; reason enough for the Dogwood Festival. It brings office workers, college students and mothers with small children into the great downtown out-of-doors for noontime concerts on street corners or in pocket parks and, of course, a big parade up Peachtree. The festival sponsors craft shows, tours of homes, and encourages people to drive through residential sections of town just to enjoy the plethora of dogwood trees at the height of their color.

Hurt Park sponsors a one-day Tulip Festival. It's the oldest of Atlanta's downtown pocket parks and this festival, dating back to 1951, is one of the city's oldest. The park, which also features a lighted fountain that changes color and spray pattern at nighttime, boasts delicately landscaped beds of tulips. The blanket of floral hues complements the rainbowed fountain. Little schoolchildren, decked out in Dutch costumes with wooden clogs, sing, dance and parade through winding paths and around a windmill erected each year just for the occasion. When the school kids aren't there, the college kids from adjacent Georgia State University use the park for their campus. They also use the fountain for fraternity pranks.

Georgia State, one of those institutions that grew right along with Atlanta, gained its university status in 1969. It started out earlier in the twentieth century as a night school division of Georgia Institute and went through several rebirths, emerging as an urban school that specialized in business and education and offered a full range of courses in all departments and divisions at hours convenient for full-time working people. It has gone on to become a full-fledged university with a student body of over 20,000, studying everything from music and art to advanced psychology to liberal arts, computer science, accounting, law and many other subjects at its urban campus.

Back in the '60s, photography students from Georgia State found an interesting place to shoot pictures behind the new Business School. They had to descend stairs from the viaducts. On dimly-lit streets they could see old storefronts which revealed lovely facades and marble columns covered with years of dirt and grime. Once in a while a truck would drive slowly by on the otherwise deserted streets to make a warehouse delivery for businesses on the street level above. Or a patrol car cruised around, just checking on things. They could follow the railroad tracks all the way three blocks over to Rich's department store on this underground route.

For nearly fifty years Atlanta's original street level had been covered over by viaducts and for the most part forgotten. That is until an enterprising group figured out that they could turn this place into Atlanta's answer to Bourbon Street and Fisherman's Wharf. Underground Atlanta polished up the marble facades on buildings that had been warehouses, filled them up with cute shops, night clubs, bars, restaurants, lit the sidewalks with gas lights and opened to the tourist trade. It was not exactly a restoration project, but still a twist for the city whose usual reaction to a building over twenty years old was to tear it down and pave a parking lot.

Visitors did come here; locals too. Underground had the monopoly on downtown entertainment, and Atlanta enjoyed a booming new night life. Unfortunately, like too many good ideas the fad faded fast; it hadn't been cultivated properly. Nearby construction on a new rapid rail transit system contributed greatly to the demise of Underground Atlanta also. Establishments like Dante Stephensen's Down the Hatch – fondues, good wine list, and excellent jazz – finally gave up the struggle to keep the Underground safe, vibrant, and attractive. So their clientele followed them to new locations out from the city's center. Underground remains shuttered amid talk and plans to revive the district and plenty of gossip about what went wrong the first time around.

Restoration not being one of Atlanta's strong points, it came as a surprise when we noticed a few brave pioneering souls buying Victorian era homes in Inman Park not far from downtown. The neighborhood had long ago gone to seed, houses divided up into multiple-family dwellings and now in a shabby condition. We had always admired these houses for what they must have been – proud, handsome structures with turrets, balconies and magnolia trees bearing over manicured lawns, the very highest elegance of that bygone era. But it seemed awfully risky to move into this neighborhood now, and to spend a lot of time and money on such a chance.

A pleasant – startling – metamorphosis: individual efforts, one an example for the next, started the transformation. Brightly painted two and three-story gingerbreads with wrap-around porches, and fenced yards festooned with flowerbeds, started changing many people's minds about saving what was left of nineteenth and early-twentieth century Atlanta. Inman Park restoration became a movement and one that worked exceedingly well. Owners who participated hung out large yellow, white and black butterfly flags, the neighborhood's symbol of its fashionable revival. In the spring – dogwood time – the neighborhood association sponsors a tour of revitalized elegant homes.

The Inman Park success, in part, encouraged a rethinking of Atlanta's community values. In the 1950s, people couldn't wait to get out of the old areas close to downtown. Then it didn't matter much to anybody if the houses that had already served several generations were torn down. But by the late 1970s the children of these same folks, kids who'd been raised with all the advantages of suburbia, found these older properties attractive for their spaciousness, location in an urban setting, and even for their age. Restoring Grant Park, West End, Midtown and other neighborhoods became major Atlanta activities, bringing along with them a renewed civic pride.

Battles to save remnants of days past haven't always been easily won; sometimes not won at all. The Trust Company of Georgia razed its old Pryor Street headquarters, an exemplary and much-admired early skyscraper; a white marble tower took its place. The old two-story Carnegie Library, that several generations of children and adults had frequented on its Carnegie Way corner, made way for the modernistic Atlanta Public Library only a few years ago.

Sometime in the '60s or '70s, when the only movie theaters still operating downtown showed X-rated films, the great Fox Theater stood closed and on the block for demolition. Southern Bell wanted to put an office tower there on Peachtree at Ponce de Leon. It took a grass roots, door-to-door, nickel-and-dime campaign that finally picked up enough support and influence to stop the outrage. At first it just wasn't a popular fight. Atlanta hadn't much experience in saving landmarks; after all both lovely old railroad stations had gone without a whimper of protest. But the Fox could admirably serve many practical purposes besides being an unusual and historic piece of architecture. Theater organists convened in Atlanta and used the Fox organ – one of the world's largest – for their performances. With demonstrations, publicity and a coalition of local support – there were many Save the Fox buttons and bumper stickers to be seen around town – the Fox now hosts national touring companies, the Atlanta Ballet's annual "Nutcracker" production, rock shows, and anyone else who wants to rent a 5,000-seat, Moorish-Egyptian auditorium with a starry ceiling. Southern Bell built its tower on an adjacent lot.

Now you would think that the world's largest chunk of exposed granite is impregnable to change. Not quite so. Before the late 1960s, Stone Mountain was a sleepy little country town famous, of course, for its unusual physical asset – the great, gray, granite mountain visible from the slightest elevation all over Atlanta. A weather-perfect Sunday afternoon often prompted a drive out to Stone Mountain for the mile climb up, a rest at the top to stare west toward Atlanta at dusk, and the easy hike back down. Citizens would take the dog along. A very uncomplicated, satisfying outing. A few other people would have the same idea and would nod a good afternoon as they trekked up the gravelly incline. Except for the climbers nobody else was around.

Then, after all those quiet years when the citizens had the mountain mostly to themselves, any time they wanted it, somebody at the State Parks Department got a bright idea. Why not put a make-believe antebellum plantation out there with Stone Mountain so people can visit the quaint old south. And a little steam railroad to go with it. People can ride it around the base of the mountain and, in case the kids get bored, some actors can stage a quaint old train hold-up scene. And they decided to make a lake so the mountain would have some nature to set it off. And a carillon so music set off nature. Someone had abandoned a carving on the face of the mountain so many years ago everyone had nearly forgotten. Better get that finished up. Since plenty of tourists would come to the new park they'd made (because they were going to advertise BIG), they let vendors in to set up hot dog and soda stands to feed them. Paved lots of lots for their cars. Even built motels for the visitors. Oh yes, a cable car in case they want to get to the top of the mountain. And a fence around it all. That's progress, Atlanta style.

The juxtaposition of tradition and progress weaves an uneven urban texture. On Saturday afternoons in October and November, inveterate fans still take their verve and enthusiasm to Georgia Tech football games. Football fever – collegiate and professional – is a chronic and incurable southern pandemic. Insatiate Atlanta added the Peach Bowl to its sports offerings a few years ago.

But other landmarks we envisioned open for time and eternity have, instead, snapped shut. Even though the Metropolitan Atlanta Rapid Transit Authority (known to everyone as MARTA) made good on their promise to whisk people conveniently into downtown on a new rail system, places we knew there have evaporated. No more blueberry muffins at the S & W Cafeteria; no more S & W. Genteel specialty shops – gone. And Atlanta's monumental Rich's department store is shrinking by the year. They just didn't have the customers they used to, so it dies a death: one department, one floor at a time.

Discussions over multi-million dollar expenditures seek to shape the future of the few remaining turn-of-the-century buildings clustered in the city's heart. The hearty few preservationists have mapped out a walking tour of the area, which includes a row of nineteenth-century stores on South Broad Street, Concordia Hall (1892) on Forsyth Street, and Flatiron Building (1897, by New York architect Bradford Gilbert), and the Healey Building (1913, now beautifully restored). A planning firm thinks it can actually attract residents to the inner city with its Fairlie-Poplar plan (named for the principal intersection on the 21-block design) of making pedestrians malls, free of cars, and creating housing for 5,000 people. A radical idea for Atlanta, bringing folks to live amid the office towers, and without automobiles! A 31.5-foot diameter neon Coca-Cola sign casts a shadow over a corner called Margaret Mitchell Square. The redevelopment plan would dismantle the giant emblem, which has perched atop a triangular-shaped building on this location for over thirty-five years, a reminder to passers-by that Atlanta is the hometown of the world-famous product.

Although appearance won't necessarily give it away, Atlanta's earliest days as the terminal point on the Western & Atlantic Railroad can be traced to this vicinity. Most Atlantans have no awareness of their city's conception and birth. Initially called Terminus, transportation patterns – first of goods, and then passengers also – determined the course of civic history. After the Civil War, when the city reconstructed its railroads, they continued to be a conduit of economic and political growth. With Atlanta as a business center the state capital relocated here from Milledgeville.

The nineteenth-century railroads selected a locus of geographic centrality. In the twentieth century, history practically repeated itself. That rickety, jerrybuilt concourse, which passed for an airport in the 1950s, soon saw the end of its service. Atlanta, along with the rest of America, moved into the jet age fast. Airlines found it a convenient spot to transfer many passengers bound for other southern destinations. Delta Air Lines even made its corporate headquarters here, and their business paralleled the city in phenomenal growth. A brand-new, aqua-colored air terminal went up, with three concourses, and by the 1960s the airport added "international" to its name. For the first time Delta grandly offered jet service direct from Atlanta to London. By the 1970s, Hartsfield International Airport handled more passengers than any airport in the country save Chicago's O'Hare. Construction on more concourses and runways rivalled activity anywhere else in town. Truly this city earned its title of Gateway to the South.

In the 1980s when we fly into Atlanta our plane taxis up beside one of the four new orange-and-tan concourse buildings that stretch out to meet hundreds of aircraft. The subdued interiors appear unremarkable except for their vast length, and the number of people milling about. Then an underground train comes along and swiftly whisks passengers away to claim their baggage at a terminal over a mile distant. A voice from some unseen source in the wall or ceiling guides us through every point of the futuristic journey. We've entered the world's largest airport. Atlanta embraces it as a symbol of times to come, experiences ahead, and the role this city intends to play in the course ahead.

We enter a place in Georgia racing to grow ahead into the future.

A picturesque view of Georgia's Pioneering territory (above) from the Appalachian Highway where cows and calves graze on lush grassland, near Blue Ridge. (Facing page) one of many splendid waterfalls situated among the mountains in Amicalola Falls State Park.

A double-barrelled cannon (top right) stands outside the well-preserved City Hall in Athens, the largest city in the Piedmont area of northeast Georgia. Remaining pictures (this page and facing page) show New Echota which had been the officially designated Cherokee capital in 1821. There are several authentically restored and reconstructed buildings in the Indian village (above and right) and the surrounding landscapes (top left and facing page) are superb.

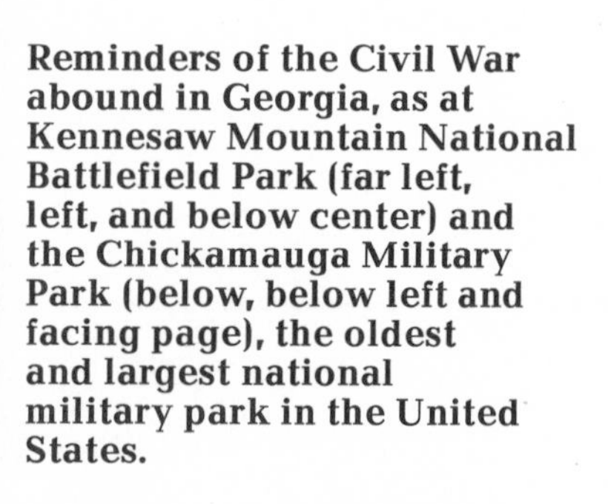

Reminders of the Civil War abound in Georgia, as at Kennesaw Mountain National Battlefield Park (far left, left, and below center) and the Chickamauga Military Park (below, below left and facing page), the oldest and largest national military park in the United States.

Warren's Mississippi Light Artillery.
2 Napoleons: 2 James.
Liddell's Brigade, Liddell's Division, Walker's Corps.
Sept. 20, 1863.
1st Lieut. H. Shannon, Commanding.
2nd Lieut. W. P. McDonald Mortally wounded.
This battery was also known as Swett's Battery. With its brigade it moved
to the extreme right in support of Gen. Breckinridge's division in the morning
and remained in position without becoming engaged till the afternoon. About
5 p.m. the battery was ordered forward by the Reed's Bridge road coming into
position on this ground on the right of its division line. When the battery opened
on the enemy about 800 yards northwest artillery from several points immediately
replied completely enfilading the line of infantry. Reynolds' division of infantry
in plain view moving at a double-quick directly against the left flank of the division
with the artillery fire above mentioned made the position untenable. The battery
was ordered to retire which it did as rapidly as possible losing one gun by the loss
of a horse which was soon after recovered by the advance of Capt. T. J. Fletcher
and a few men of the 13th Arkansas. Casualties of the battle: killed 2 enlisted
men wounded 1 officer 8 enlisted men 11 horses killed or disabled.

Towering skyscrapers, a golden domed Capitol, neon advertisements and a complex network of freeways are lit at night and provide Atlanta City with a glittering spectacle (right). Martin Luther King, the eloquent black Baptist minister who led the mass civil rights movement in the U.S. from the 1950s, was born in Atlanta, and although he was assassinated in Memphis, Tennessee, the marble tomb in his honor has been placed in his birthplace (above).

FLY DELTA

Atlanta is the capital of Georgia and the state's largest city. It has also become a big league sports city since the completion in April 1965 of the Stadium (above). The beautiful, domed and columned Capitol building (facing page) gracing Downtown Atlanta (overleaf) symbolizes the spirit of this majestic city.

Skyscrapers soar impressively to meet the early morning sky in Downtown Atlanta (above) and dwarf trees and fountains in Hurt Park (facing page), where office workers can while away lunch hours free from the bustle of the city.

EQUITABLE

Manifestations of contemporary culture dominate views of Downtown Atlanta, ranging from a statue of local baseball record-breaker, 'Hank' Aaron (above), to modern architecture (remaining pictures).

The Classic Renaissance style of the Capitol (above) adds a brightness to the Atlanta skyline and a contrast to the modern High Museum of Art (facing page) or towering skyscrapers (overleaf left). The Capitol's dome shines with gold and supports a statue of 'Miss Freedom', in memory of Georgia's war dead (overleaf right).

EQUITABLE

Within the calm, elegant grounds of the Capitol stands a replica of the Statue of Liberty (above). One of the few husband-and-wife statues in the world is that of Civil War Governor and Mrs. Joseph Emerson Brown (overleaf right). Meanwhile, Downtown Atlanta continues at its busy pace (facing page and overleaf left).

MUSE'S
REGAL SHOE
BRINKS
PITTSTON
TRAL CITY PARK
ITY OF ATLANTA

MUSES
EASTERN
marta

Two entirely dissimilar museum houses are situated on Atlanta's 25-acre historical society complex: (below) Tullie Smith House and (bottom left) Swan House. (Bottom right) Governor's Mansion, (left) Atlanta University and (facing page) Atlanta at dusk.

EQUITABLE

The 90 feet high and 190 feet wide Stone Mountain Memorial Carving (top right) was completed in 1970. A scenic railroad passes around the base of the mountain and full gauge replicas of Civil War locomotives travel upon its line (top left). (Left and above) plantation huts in Stone Mountain Park and Battlefield Park respectively.

HALL

The clock dome atop the City Hall in Athens (previous page) is a repeated design on the Barrow County Court House (left) in Winder, west of Athens. Georgia State University's gleaming white buildings are also found in the Athens (below and bottom pictures), as is Church Waddel Brumby House (facing page).

A dusty trail leads to a village (above and facing page, top left) near Madison. Morgan County Courthouse (facing page, top right and bottom pictures) is situated in Madison – the heart of Dixie.

GEORGIA
1776
MORGAN COUNTY
Morgan County was created by Act of Dec. 10, 1807 from Baldwin County. It was named for Gen. Daniel Morgan (1736-1802), a native of N. J. "Exactly fitted for the toils and pomp of war," he served with distinction on Benedict Arnold's expedition to Quebec in 1775-6, commanded the riflemen at Saratoga in 1777 and defeated Tarleton at Cowpens in 1781. After the War he served two terms in Congress. First county officers of Morgan County, commissi
d January 14, 1808, were: Joseph White,
John Nesbitt, Clk. Sup. Ct.; Isham S.
Clk. Inf. Ct.; Daniel Sessions, Surveyor;
HISTORICAL COMMISSION

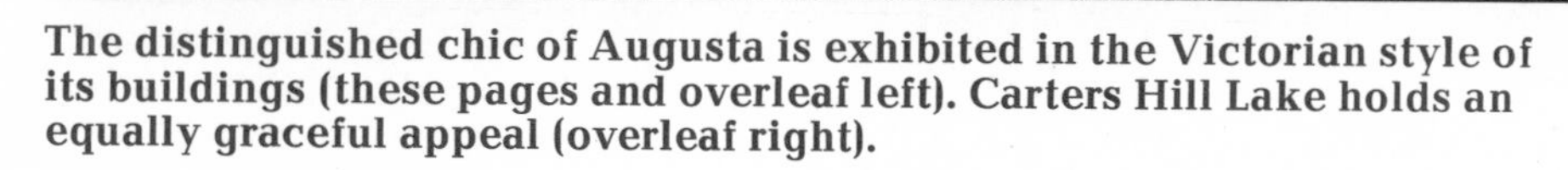

The distinguished chic of Augusta is exhibited in the Victorian style of its buildings (these pages and overleaf left). Carters Hill Lake holds an equally graceful appeal (overleaf right).

404

Milledgeville boasts many examples of Southern mansions, such as the Old Governor's Mansion (top), Stetson-Sanford House (facing page), Georgia Military Institute (right) and Georgia College (above and top right).

STETSON-SANFORD
HOUSE
CIRCA 1820
ONE OF THE FINEST
EXAMPLES OF
FEDERAL PERIOD
ARCHITECTURE
RESTORATION BY
OLD CAPITAL
HISTORICAL SOCIETY

The Jarrell Plantation is situated in the Juliette vicinity. Its agricultural complex has been preserved as a typical Middle Georgia farm (above). Macon lies at the very center of Georgia on each side of the Ocmulgee River. Within its boundaries, Ocmulgee National Monument retains the burial mounds of the early Creeks (facing page) and is an important prehistoric site.

Columned buildings are frequently seen in Georgia – Macon (above) is no exception with its refined, pillared Mercer University (facing page, top and bottom left and overleaf left); elegant Hay House (facing page, top right and overleaf right) and Federal Courthouse (facing page, bottom right).

FEDERAL BUILDING AND U.S. COURT HOUSE

Columbus has preserved a 19th century character to its city. Tree-lined streets, pleasant parks and beautiful gardens, such as Gallaway Gardens (facing page, top left, bottom left and right), create a picturesque setting. The historic district of Columbus contains majestic houses which add color and grandeur to the old frontier settlement (this page and facing page, top right).

As these pages illustrate, Georgia's "Little Grand Canyon" has spectacular erosion gullies up to 150 feet deep, situated in Providence Canyon State Park.

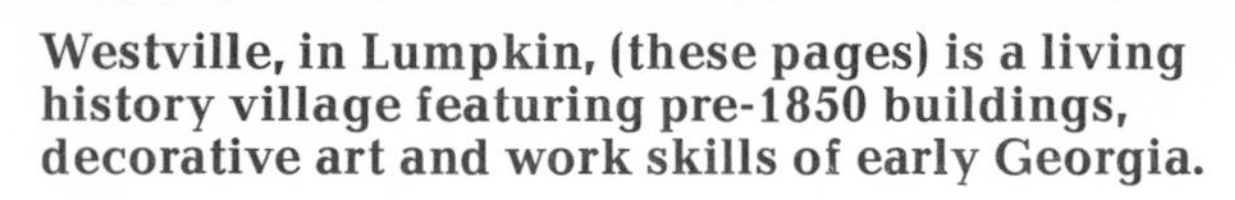

Westville, in Lumpkin, (these pages) is a living history village featuring pre-1850 buildings, decorative art and work skills of early Georgia.

Plaques at Fort Gaines, in Clay County, give details of the site's history, while the houses in the area also reflect the Fort's past (these pages).

GEORGIA
1776
CLAY COUNTY
This County created by Act of the Legislature Feb. 16, 1854, is named for Henry Clay, famous statesman who died in 1852. Near Fort Gaines, the County Site, stood the actual Fort built in 1816 for defense in the Creek Indian Wars and named for Gen. Edmond P. Gaines who ordered its construction. Among the first County Officers were: Sheriff George R. Holloway, Clerk of the Superior & Inferior Courts Warren Sutton, Ordinary John H. Jones, Tax Receiver John H. Gilbert, Tax Collector Peter Lee, County Surveyor Bennett H. Thornton and Coroner Churchill Patrick.
GEORGIA
1776
FORT GAINES GUARDS
Organized in 1836 under the command of Col. J. E. Brown, for 74 years the Fort Gaines Guards was one of the best and, later, the oldest military organization in western Georgia. Kept intact between wars, the Guards fought in the Indian and Mexican Wars. In 1861, 120 men under Capt. B. A. Turnipseed, as Co. D, 9th Ga. Regiment, Tige Anderson's Brigade, Longstreet's Corps, fought gallantly through the War Between the States. Of the original 120, only 13 remained to surrender at Appomattox. Reorganized in 1868, a detachment of the Guards under Lt. E. A. Greene, volunteered for service in 1898 in the Spanish-American War. The Guards were disbanded about 1910.
GEORGIA HISTORICAL COMMISSION

Swamplands (above) lie south of semi-tropical Albany and are also found (facing page) near the tobacco-producing city of Tifton.

Americus flourished in the 1890s and a number of elegant Victorian-Gothic buildings remain (this page and facing page, top left). Plains has acquired its name from the nine miles of fertile plains which feature in the region (facing page, bottom right) and is home-town of 39th President Carter, whose headquarters are shown (facing page, bottom left and top right).

PLAINS, GEORGIA
JIMMY CARTER

During the Civil War, Andersonville was the death site of nearly 13,000 Union prisoners. The graves of Union soldiers and other veterans are in the Andersonville National Cemetery, which has many monuments erected by states whose sons are buried here (these pages).

"WE HERE HIGHLY RESOLVE THAT THESE DEAD SHALL NOT HAVE DIED IN VAIN—THAT THIS NATION, UNDER GOD, SHALL HAVE A NEW BIRTH OF FREEDOM—AND THAT GOVERNMENT OF THE PEOPLE, BY THE PEOPLE, FOR THE PEOPLE, SHALL NOT PERISH FROM THE EARTH."
(GETTYSBURG ADDRESS)
ABRAHAM LINCOLN.
ERECTED BY THE
STATE OF ILLINOIS
IN GRATEFUL REMEMBRANCE OF THE PATRIOTIC DEVOTION OF HER SONS WHO SUFFERED AND DIED IN THE MILITARY PRISON AT ANDERSONVILLE, GA.
1864 — 1865
"THE MYSTIC CHORDS OF MEMORY, STRETCHING FROM EVERY BATTLEFIELD AND PATRIOT GRAVE TO EVERY LIVING HEART AND HEARTHSTONE ALL OVER THIS BROAD LAND, WILL YET SWELL THE CHORUS OF THE UNION, WHEN AGAIN TOUCHED, AS SURELY THEY WILL BE, BY THE BETTER ANGELS OF OUR NATURE."
(FIRST INAUGURAL ADDRESS)
ABRAHAM LINCOLN.

Scenes in Georgia Veterans Memorial State Park (above and facing page), where swimming, boating, waterskiing, and other outdoor sports are held.

Situated in southern Georgia, Agrirama (these pages) exemplifies the simple, rustic life which still prevails in much of the state.

Lapham-Patterson House is a restored, three-story Victorian mansion (these pages), situated in Thomasville, South Georgia. Its splendid structure is underlined with detailed exterior decoration (facing page) and tasteful furnishings (above). East of Thomasville, Okefenokee State Park contrasts the sedate mansion with murky swamps (overleaf pages).

With the ominous presence of alligators (right) in the swamplands of Okefenokee State Park (overleaf pages), a boardwalk (above and top right) is a welcoming sight to those crossing the marshy forests. Nearby Laura S. Walker State Park possesses clearer waters (left).

Okefenokee State Park swamps (previous pages) occupy an area of 700 square miles. Termed "land of trembling earth" by Creek Indians, its lakes of dark brown water are fed by streams leading from the Suwannee River. On these pages is shown the charm of coastal St. Marys, situated southeast of the swamps.

Reached by causeway from Brunswick, tiny Jekyll Island has retained many of the luxurious 'cottages' (these pages and overleaf) which were originally owned by millionaires; J. P. Morgan's cottage (top left) and Rockefeller's cottage (top right and overleaf right) are just two examples.

CENTER FOR THE
CREATIVE ARTS
JEKYLL ISLAND
ARTS
GARDEN
CLUB

Hofwyl-Broadfield Plantation is a pleasant part of a nature trail with tranquil views of rural life (this page). St. Simons Island lies northeast of the plantation and its present lighthouse and coastal guard's house (facing page) are landmarks.

St. Simons Island is the site of the Lovely Lane Chapel (top right) and of Christ Church, Frederica (facing page) which was built for the first congregation in Oglethorpe's settlement. The remaining pictures (this page) portray remnants of General Oglethorpe's fort.

Fort Mc Allister (these pages) was built in 1861 and was the southernmost fortification that guarded Savannah's coast (overleaf pages) from attack by sea, although the fort fell on December 13, 1864, after 15 minutes of desperate hand-to-hand combat.

KEEP OFF

HENRY SIMS MORGAN
2D LIEUTENANT
CORPS OF ENGINEERS
CLASS OF 1897
U. S. MILITARY ACADEMY
BORN OCTOBER 14, 1874
DROWNED AUGUST 31, 1898
WHILE ATTEMPTING TO RESCUE THE CREW
OF BARK NOE WRECKED IN TYBEE ROADS
ERECTED BY HIS CLASSMATES

Major restoration efforts have ensured that Savannah is one of the most beautiful and historically interesting cities in the South. It has handsome architecture within spacious squares and streets (these pages) which were conceived by General Oglethorpe, who was inspired by Robert Castell's sketch entitled *Villas of the Ancients*. **Previous pages depict views of Fort Pulaski, Savannah, which was named after Count Casimir Pulaski, who was killed there in battle.**

ANDREW LOW HOUSE
CLOSED THURSDAYS

Savannah's old houses (top left and left) provide an interesting contrast to the more ornate architecture of wrought iron work and classical columns which pervade the city's buildings (above). Juliette Gordon Low's birthplace (facing page) the bright stucco of the Pink House (overleaf right) and the Regency-style house (overleaf left) illustrate striking examples of elaborate design.

The Olde Pink House
RESTAURANT & TAVERN
JOHN WESLEY'S
AMERICAN PARISH - SAVANNAH
Wesley, an Anglican minister, served as the religious leader of the Georgia colony from February 6, 1736 to December 2, 1737. Seeking to minister to all, he led services in English, French, German, Spanish, and Italian.
Honor was accorded John Wesley, founder of Methodism, and this New World area where he lived and worked, by the declaration of the 1976 United Methodist General Conference that his "American Parish" be a United Methodist National Historic Landmark.
The landmark encompasses:
JOHN
WESLEY
1703–1791
FOUNDER
OF
METHODISM
MINISTER
OF THE
CHURCH OF ENGLAND
IN SAVANNAH
1736–1737
MY HEART'S DESIRE
FOR THIS PLACE
IS NOT THAT IT BE
A FAMOUS OR A RICH
BUT THAT IT MAY BE
A RELIGIOUS COLONY
AND THEN I AM SURE
IT CANNOT FAILE
OF THE
BLESSING OF GOD

INDEX

DLB.34103-84